T0123794

You Are Wonderfully COMPLEX

Use Your Words to Design and Build Your World-Changing Future

Lester K.A. Cox

YOU ARE WONDERFULLY COMPLEX
USE YOUR WORDS TO DESIGN AND BUILD
YOUR WORLD-CHANGING FUTURE

iUniverse books may be ordered through booksellers or by contacting:

iUniverse
1663 Liberty Drive
Bloomington, IN 47403
www.iuniverse.com
1-800-Authors (1-800-288-4677)

ISBN: 978-1-5320-0777-4 (sc)
ISBN: 978-1-5320-0776-7 (e)

Library of Congress Control Number: 2016917386

Print information available on the last page.

iUniverse rev. date: 12/13/2016

Contents

PART 1

Value Awareness and Spin-Off Benefits

PART 2

Wake Up and Take Action

PART 3
Discover and Share

I am deeply grateful to my parents, Philip J. and Sybil K. Cox, who planted the incorruptible seed and so many other productive seeds in my life.

Preface

THE TEAM I LED HAD just undergone a departmental restructuring, resulting in the loss of employment of several team members. Over the years, this team had bonded well together, and close friendships had developed; the reality of the downsizing was therefore understandably upsetting.

In a morning meeting on the day the restructuring took effect, I encouraged the team to be supportive of one another and attentive to their spoken words. At that time, it had started to become apparent to me that words spoken had the potential to build up or tear down; ultimately, everyone had a choice in the selection of his or her words.

My leadership and change-management group encouraged me to stay close to the team and think of ways to encourage and inspire them. My search for ways to demonstrate concern for my team gave birth to my sending out weekly inspirational messages to the team first thing on Monday mornings. At the outset, I'd thought these messages would continue for just a few weeks since I did not consider myself a writer. Many team members thanked me repeatedly for sharing words that resonated well with them, spurred them to step outside of their comfort zones, gave them a sense of hope, and liberated them to take responsibility for their own destinies. These messages continued for sixty-five weeks and ended just prior to my departure from the unit.

In the first message, a lumberjack showed how enormous trees were more valuable when they grew together in groves as opposed to in isolation, even if they were massive and supremely towered over all the other trees. The lumberjack suggested that while the isolated tree might appear to do quite well and produce a lot of lumber, this lumber was not valuable. This could seem a bit contradictory, especially to some superstars and highfliers. However, the wise lumberjack explained that because of the overwhelming number of branches on the taller trees growing in isolation, when the trees are cut and sawed, they would have a lot of knots. The greater number of knots, the lower the value. The higher-quality lumber cuts were clear with no knots.

My final weekly message to the team encouraged them to choose to bloom wherever they were planted. This message highlighted the power of perception and choice. It made reference to one of three bricklayers' response to renowned architect Sir Christopher Wren's question regarding what they were doing as they were working on the reconstruction of Saint Paul's Cathedral in London. One bricklayer chose to view his involvement not as a simple bricklayer but as creator of a magnificent cathedral. Somewhat similar to how the bricklayer was able to visualize the magnificent cathedral, in 2015, inmates at a correctional facility in Philadelphia saw Pope Francis's visit as an opportunity to craft and present him with a magnificent chair.

When seeds are planted, they do not have a choice as to where they are planted—they cannot get up once planted and go elsewhere. While seeds have kinetic energy, they bloom where they are planted. Energy is inside the seed. This energy on the inside has the power to sprout the most productive trees—if the conditions are right. By the same token, this energy could produce the most vexing, irritating plants and trees—if the conditions are right. Words are similar to seeds in many respects; they bloom where they are planted.

As the leader planted in a heartrending situation, I dug deep inside and mustered up internal energy that gave life to fruitful gifts—words. What do you do when you have gifts? You share them with others; you use these gifts to serve others. I had responsibility for my team's well-being and considered it a privilege to help them grow and achieve personal fulfillment by sharing uplifting words.

A fulfilling life is intrinsically linked to the quality of your heart and spirit, which represent the soil in which these words are planted. This book has been written to raise consciousness of the power of your own words and those of others; more importantly, this book's objective is to inspire and empower you to choose to speak productively and enhance the quality of your interior soil. Why is the latter point so important even though many seasoned farmers state that the seed is the master of the soil? Because once words enter your soul and find the right conditions, they take over and become your masters.

Opening Words

MANY PEOPLE MISS ODD-DEFYING AND positive life-changing opportunities primarily because of a surprisingly simple reason. Search, rescue, and emergency responder teams know this fundamental reason well because it quickly increases their chances of success. The genuine millionaires next door, who have achieved financial freedom, learned this reason early in their lives. They are the neighbors who drive quality, economical cars and lead comparably simple lifestyles. Walt Disney, Dwight D. Eisenhower, Carl Sandburg, Martin Luther King Jr., John Wayne, Tom Brokaw, Jackie Robinson, Wayne Gretzky, and Warren Buffet were all newspaper carriers early in their lives, and they fully appreciated this simple reason.

People who truly experience meaningful lives and notably impact the lives of many others realize that all great achievements have humble beginnings. That's it. These people do not chase the next lottery jackpot or fastidiously wait for their knights in shining armor. Rather, they understand that huge results grow from making many incremental changes over time.

You might be thinking that you do not have the time to wait for small changes to manifest based on where you are now and where you want to be. You would perhaps prefer real results sooner rather than later. If I could share ways to trigger a chain reaction that produces and reproduces true happiness and fulfillment, would you make the time investment now?

Former prime minister of the United Kingdom (1874–1880) Benjamin Disraeli captures my intentions for you when he said, "The greatest good you can do for another is not just to share your riches, but to reveal to him his own."

At the end of every chapter, I will ask you to reflect on the contents. These reflections are intended to have you switch on the light and face the mirror to reveal your true value and new possibilities.

I will make a case for you to take advantage of a powerful force at your disposal, a force that can change your life experiences for the better. If you desire world-changing fulfillment in your life, dive in and spur one of the most worthwhile investments in yourself!

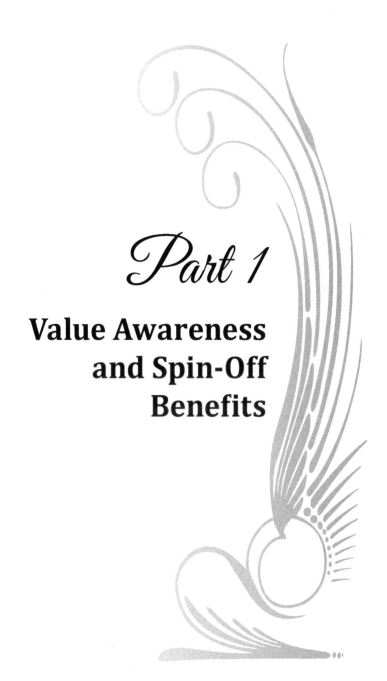

Part 1

Value Awareness and Spin-Off Benefits

Chapter 1
Priceless

The promises of this world are, for the most part, vain phantoms; and to confide in one's self, and become something of worth and value is the best and safest course.
—Michelangelo

Y OUR NAME MAY NOT BE featured on any of the lists of the world's richest people because no one on earth can figure out your value. This is in spite of the fact that you have more than thirty-seven trillion in your possession! How can one person have so much? They continue to divide, conquer, and grow. This number far exceeds the minimum starting points for many of the lists of wealth; in 2015, the starting point for the Forbes 400 list was $1.7 billion.[1]

You may have already guessed that I am referring to the uncountable number of cells in your body—the basic yet complex units of the human body.[2] Please follow my argument regarding your value.

There are many ways appraisers go about establishing the value of someone or something. Fundamentally, a few factors they consider are the difference between what is owned and what is owed, usefulness, the amount someone else is willing to pay, and what is provided in exchange. Should you consider your body cells in this light, the picture of your value would start to emerge. Cells are useful in taking in nutrients, converting them to energy, reproducing, growing, and producing essential proteins. If you desperately needed cells and they were available to you, how much would you pay for them? As an indication, the cost of stem cell therapy, which provides master cells that can grow into any of the body's cell types, vary widely between $9,000 and $60,000 per treatment.[3] Given the complexity of the treatment and early stage of its scientific development, stem cell therapy is still not widely available.

Sometimes the value of something escalates because it is rare and hard to exactly reproduce. In other words, the higher the rarity, the higher the value.

Your fingerprint: the chance that it will match someone else's is one in approximately sixty-four million.

Your iris: the chance of any two matching is one in about seven billion.

As you ponder your great value, I want you to recognize another valuation principle: the higher the complexity, the higher the value. Shrewd researchers and strategists who want to remain on the cutting edge or ahead of their competition recognize complexity as a highly valuable quality, especially when it is relevant. A broad range of designers and performers strive to master and display complexity because of the valuable accolades that follow as a result.

This is how a Yahoo sportswriter captured how twenty-six seconds of complex performance routines changed the world: "Flying from the low bar to the high one and back again five different times, Comaneci showed off an artistry that had never been seen before. And when her routine was over—when she stuck the landing after a full flip and a half twist, a dismount only she could do ..."[4]

Olympic history was made in 1976 when fourteen-year-old Romanian Nadia Comaneci executed a perfect routine on the uneven bars. If the Swiss luxury watchmaker Omega had really known the determination of this little girl, it would have manufactured the scoreboard to reflect four digits. According to a later report in the *Guardian*, a director of the watch company said, "I was told a 10.00 is not possible."[5] Evidently young Nadia was not told of this impossibility. She began her gymnastics journey in kindergarten, and after breaking many of her family couches and eight hours of training, six days a week, she achieved, on the world Olympics stage, gymnastics' first perfect score of 10.00—initially displayed as 1.00. In all, she has been awarded seven scores of 10.00 and remains the youngest all-around champion in Olympic history.

The higher the complexity, the higher the value. Take note that your wonderful complexity was masterfully created during the embryonic or prenatal stage of your development. Werner Gitt, a former engineering professor at the National Metrology Institute of Germany, examined and summarized with wonder only one of your body's information processing abilities as follows:

> Without a doubt, the most complex information-processing system in existence is the human body. If we take all human information processes together, i.e. conscious ones (language,

information-controlled, deliberate voluntary movements) and unconscious ones (information-controlled functions of the organs, hormone system), this involves the processing of 10^{24} bits daily. This astronomically high figure is higher by a factor of 1,000,000 [i.e., is a million times greater] than the total human knowledge of 10^{18} bits stored in all the world's libraries.[6]

While you are one person, your entire worth has an inestimable independent value. In short, you are priceless and wonderfully complex!

Value Creation

First impressions are *not* everything. Some of you may have given up on your dreams because you made a poor first impression. You *only* had one shot, and you blew it. Let's return to Nadia Comaneci. She placed thirteenth in her *first* Romania national championships in 1969! Just imagine if she had given up because of this "bad" first impression.

First impressions are just that; you have subsequent opportunities to make lasting impressions. When the great Italian sculptor Michelangelo first saw the single slab of marble, he knew it was not everything. He saw an opportunity to sculpt a young and beautiful mother serenely cradling and mourning over the body of her dead son. In 1499, he created the *Pietà* statue. The exquisite attention to detail was so impressive that well-respected Italian painter, architect, writer, and historian Giorgio Vasari wrote the following about the inscription on the diagonal sash draped across the mother's body.

Here is perfect sweetness in the expression of the head, harmony in the joints and attachments of the arms, legs, and trunk, and the pulses and veins so wrought, that in truth Wonder herself must marvel that the hand of a craftsman should have been able to execute so divinely and so perfectly, in so short a time, a work so admirable; and it is certainly a miracle that a stone without any shape at the beginning should ever have been reduced to such perfection as Nature is scarcely able to create in the flesh.[7]

This is reportedly the only work upon which Michelangelo attached his name for an unmistakable lasting impression. Today, the Pietà is protected behind a bulletproof glass panel at Saint Peter's Basilica in Vatican City and is considered to be priceless.

The two figures in Michelangelo's monumental work formed the shape of a pyramid. You too can create impressive value with the symbolic stability of the triangles that make up the pyramid. In the next chapter, I unveil how you can start to choose to exploit the power of your invaluable *you* and cause "Wonder herself" to marvel.

Wonder, Appreciation, and Reflection

Recap

The very essence, uniqueness, and complexity of your physical structure point to your inestimable value. By discovering your innate value, you can achieve seemingly impossible feats and creatively shape your future in impressive ways.

Reflection

Think back on a time in your life when you received a sincere compliment that made you feel valuable. Did you put a price tag on it (e.g., it was worth fifty dollars, a hundred dollars, etc.)? I believe such compliments are priceless.

To create lasting impressions, the next time you receive such compliments,

- express gratitude,
- humbly affirm them to yourself, and
- convert them to positive energy and deposit them in your value account.

Notes

_____
_____
_____
_____
_____
_____
_____
_____
_____
_____
_____
_____
_____
_____
_____
_____
_____
_____
_____
_____
_____
_____
_____
_____
_____
_____
_____
_____

Chapter 2

World-Class Potential

Small opportunities are often the beginning of great enterprises.

—Demosthenes

YOU CAN ABSOLUTELY BECOME A wonder of the world, a remarkable person in this world. Within each of you are implanted latent wonders awaiting the right conditions to spring forth to make you a better person and this world a better place. If you are already a wonder of the world, this book will help you keep your distinction by creating new, more, and better value!

The Power of One: Small Start, Big Finish

Many marvels of this world can be traced back to humble beginnings. Let us now consider the Seven Wonders of the Ancient World:[1]

1. The Great Pyramid of Giza
2. The Hanging Gardens of Babylon
3. The Statue of Zeus at Olympia
4. The Temple of Artemis at Ephesus
5. The Mausoleum at Halicarnassus
6. The Colossus of Rhodes
7. The Lighthouse of Alexandria

The oldest and only one that still exists today is the Great Pyramid of Giza. Located in Egypt, after twenty years of hard work, this structure was completed in 2560 BC and stands at 146.5 meters (481 feet) high or the equivalent of a forty-eight-story building. Up to 2010, the Great Pyramid of Giza held the title as the tallest man-made structure. It took approximately 2.3 million blocks to construct the pyramid. After preparing the rock base of over thirteen acres, the construction started with *just one* stone block.

Palatial Living

The World Heritage Convention (WHC), an organization of the United Nations Educational, Scientific, and Cultural Organization (UNESCO), keeps a keen eye out for man-made wondrous structures or sites of outstanding international significance and then designates them as World Heritage Sites.

In 2001, the WHC designated a town overlooking the Dead Sea Valley, the Judean Desert, and Masada in Israel as a World

Heritage Site.[2] This fortress of Masada was where Herod the Great constructed luxurious palaces and other supporting buildings in 30 BCE. Today, Masada is Israel's most popular paid tourist attraction.

Well-renowned Israeli archaeologist, Dr. Yigael Yadin, spearheaded excavations at Masada between 1963 and 1965 and discovered a treasure trove of artifacts, including more than six thousand pottery vessels and botanical seeds. The seeds were considered the *least valuable* of the discoveries and were stored at the Bar-Ilan University in Tel Aviv for forty years.

Right Conditions

In 2005, a few of the seeds were forwarded to the University of Zurich for radiocarbon dating, and the results revealed that the seeds were approximately two thousand years old. Three seeds from the discovery were given to plant specialist, Dr. Elaine Solowey, and she carefully planted them in soil on January 19, 2005.

On June 12, 2005, the *New York Times* published "After 2,000 Years, a Seed from Ancient Judea Sprouts." Prior to planting the seeds in new soil, "she first soaked the seeds in hot water to soften the coat, then in an acid rich in hormones, then in an enzymatic fertilizer made of seaweed and other nutrients."[3]

The sheltered embryo within the seed had its internal food supply intact, and it awoke from its long rest when the conditions were right. Six weeks later, Dr. Solowey was delighted to see life emerging from the soil.

While the seeds may have seemed to be the least valuable of the Masada discoveries, *one* seed became the world's oldest seed to germinate.[4]

The Power of Zero and One

Two digits have revolutionized our world: zero and one. The World Wide Web, a global communication network of computers, had 3.6 billion users as of June 30, 2016. It exchanges and processes information fundamentally using only these two numbers.[5] By storing data and performing calculations simply using zeros and ones, tremendous power is readily at the disposal of many users, far beyond the imagination of its inventors.

You can change your world by appreciating that simplicity and ordinary dispositions represent building blocks and stepping-stones for you to achieve world-class results. Best-selling authors Gary Keller and Jay Papasan shared a similar view by suggesting that you can make substantial progress when you focus on the small but vital building blocks of your dreams and desires. They encapsulated this concept in this manner: "Going small is a simple approach to extraordinary results, and it works. It works all the time, anywhere and on anything."[6]

Wonder, Appreciation, and Reflection

Recap

It is important to realize that all great accomplishments have humble beginnings. Oftentimes, this humility cloaks world-class potential that can be unleashed under the right conditions and with the appropriate focus.

Reflection

Consider one thing, no matter how simple, that you do or did well. How did you feel when you started to hit your stride and make good progress with this?

- Believe in yourself. Remind yourself often of the power of one and the amazing growth that could result from the connection to and with one.
- One spark ... warming fire.
- One drop ... energetic ripples.
- One seed ... one fruit ... one tree ... one forest.
- What one "sleeping" desire, if awakened right now, could ripple out to create new and exciting opportunities for you?

Notes

_____

_____

_____

_____

_____

_____

_____

_____

_____

_____

_____

_____

_____

_____

_____

_____

_____

_____

_____

_____

_____

_____

_____

_____

_____

Chapter 3

New Beginnings

So never lose an opportunity of urging a practical beginning, however small, for it is wonderful how often in such matters the mustard-seed germinates and roots itself.

—Florence Nightingale

I N ADDITION TO THE INTERIOR food supply, a typical seed is made up of an embryo (a new beginning or undeveloped state) and a seed coat (outer protective covering). The embryo is in a state of suspension and in its comfort zone. In this state, nothing happens if nothing happens. This might explain, in part, the survival of the Masada seed. Does this sound familiar? Same old, same old.

Nothing seems to get you out of the doldrums? Some seeds have gone through difficult times and been exposed to hostile environments. They have toughened up and built walls around themselves. In other words, all the "stuff" going on outside of the seed is prevented from permeating its hardened coat.

Let us observe how the embryo gets out of the doldrums and starts growing.

- *Softening of the protective coating.* As indicated in chapter 2, one of the first actions Dr. Solowey reportedly took was soaking the two-thousand-year-old seeds in hot water, hormones, and fertilizer to promote the softening of the seed coat. For the seed to develop into a plant, the coat had to be broken.

- *Placement in good soil.* Once the embryo is awakened, it starts consuming the internal food supply quickly. Planting the seed in soil that is rich in organic matter and nutrients is important since the internal food supply is limited and is exhausted rapidly once the embryo is awakened. This soil serves as a new source of food and shelter for the plant.

- *Establishment of a firm anchor.* The first external sign of this survival is when the root breaks through the seed coat into the soil, providing food and foundation, as it anchors the embryo.

Multiplier Effect

One morning after cutting a papaya in half, one of my daughters asked about the black round things inside the fleshy fruit. I explained that they were seeds and then came a barrage of questions! How many seeds are there? Can you eat them? Can you plant them?

Can you plant them? Yes. Let them dry out, plant them, and within seven to eleven months, you could have a massive papaya farm. Invariably, the seed is going to reproduce itself.

The thought of lots of little papayas had my mind racing. One papaya has about five hundred seeds, so this can yield potentially five hundred plants. Each papaya plant can produce up to 150 papayas per year (it bears fruit year-round). Therefore, one papaya can produce an astounding 75,000 papayas in one year. With a productive life span of five years, one papaya has the potential of producing a whopping 375,000 papayas or 187.5 million seeds!

Compare this productive amplitude to redwood trees, which are the tallest trees in the world (369 feet). A mature tree (between five and fifteen years old) produces approximately ten million seeds per year in cones, and many of the trees have life spans of two thousand years. I will let you determine the multiplier effect of one of their seeds.

Reproduction

Essentially, a seed is a unit of reproduction that goes from a seeming state of latent dormancy to dependence and then interdependence in order to be productive. The awakening of life within the Masada seed sparked new beginnings and brought to mind a few other new beginnings in history that have similar multiplier effects.

- When the conditions are right, corporations, institutions, cities, and nations are born. Beforehand, the individuals involved would engage in dialogue, and then once there is agreement, constitutions or other written instruments are prepared to confirm the new beginnings. Many of these corporations, institutions, cities, and nations go on to spend money to buy products or services or support others; these produce many spin-off effects in the economy.

- Couples firm up their relationships by marriage; vows are exchanged in a ceremony, and a written certificate is issued for validation. Many have children who in turn have more children.

- Teams and impressive movements have been germinated with the willing response to words such as: "Follow me," "One for all, all for one," "One man, one vote," "Power to the people," "Equal pay for equal work," "The personal is political," "Make love, not war," "We shall overcome," "Je suis Charlie," and "We are the 99 percent."

A common thread emerged from these new beginnings—dialogue and then a constitution or a written document. A word, similar to a seed, is also a unit; it is a unit of language that has the potential to reproduce. A word has the capacity to respond to the environment, grow, consume energy, and reproduce. Words written thousands of years ago, when read today, come out of their protective covers and come alive from their dormancy. Many of you may have experienced this with poems or other literary works. It is as if the words sprouted off the page to come alive in your hearts—and you very likely share your enthusiasm or influence with others.

Multiplier Effect—Revisited

As with the papaya seeds, if words produce after their kind and have the ability to multiply, what could this mean? On average, adults speak about sixteen thousand words per day, according to a study completed by Professor Matthias Mehl of the University of Arizona.[1]

Depending on the conditions, results could potentially start sprouting fairly quickly after these words are spoken. You might conclude that some words really do not mean much by themselves, and I would agree, but in context, many could definitely produce certain effects. Years ago, when training two of our German shepherds, I gave commands in French even though we were living in a country where English was predominant. The dogs responded appropriately to these commands/sounds and connected the context. These sounds became "words" for the dogs because of repetition and their connections to specific events or objects (reward with biscuits or praising words).

You Attach Meanings to Words

What about self-talk (words spoken quietly or loudly to yourself). "I can do this! This is going to be a great day!" What would be the impact if the words you spoke in one day were to all bear fruit like the papaya seeds? For illustration purposes, let's briefly explore the potential outcome using the same criteria for the papaya seed (each of your sixteen thousand words spoken daily produces 150 fruits per year, bearing fruit all year round with a five-year life span): 2.4 million *fruits* in one year and 12 million *fruits* in five years!

According to the *Oxford Dictionary*, *fruits* refer to "the result or reward of work or activity." In archaic usage, they are called "offspring."[2] This latter definition requires us to go back to a few points made regarding the "offspring" of a seed it produces (papaya seeds produce papaya plants and fruits).

Ultimately, what *fruits* are coming from your words? More importantly, what is the multiplier effect of your *fruits*, which contain the words to produce more *fruits*?

All words are not created equally. Broadly speaking, words are positive, negative, or neutral.

Not too long ago, we had a water treatment and filtration system installed in our home. Prior to installation, the purification expert explained that we knowing and unknowingly take in the chemicals and sediments from water. The expert filled two small glasses from our kitchen faucet and asked me to swirl my finger in the glass for about thirty seconds. When he tested both glasses of water for chlorine, the one in which I swirled my finger had very little chlorine compared to the untouched glass of water. What happened? My finger actually absorbed the chlorine. This freaked me out a little since I love long, warm showers. I was drinking the chemical in the water, my largest organ (the skin) was absorbing it, and my lungs were inhaling it in its vaporized form.

Be careful not to absorb words that are not to your benefit. This is particularly important since human beings tend to speak more negative words than other types of words. According to Penn State University's professor of applied linguistics, Dr. Robert W. Schrauf, "People know more negative emotion words than positive or neutral words. The proportion of words was 50 percent negative, 30 percent positive, and 20 percent neutral." Dr. Schrauf concluded that negative words are more mentally taxing on individuals. "Negative emotions trigger detailed process distinctions, nuances and, consequently, more words."[3]

Let's revisit the potential 2.4 million "fruits" produced per year from words spoken in a single day. Once a seed or word is awakened from dormancy, it will *only* produce after itself. This means positive words will produce positive results, and negative words will produce negative results. A breakdown of the 2.4 million "fruits" using the research results of Dr. Schrauf would likely be 1.2 million *negative* fruits, 720,000 *positive* fruits, and 480,000 *neutral* fruits.

Wonder, Appreciation, and Reflection

Recap

While the seed coat serves as protection, for growth to occur, conducive changes in the seed conditions must take place. These changes set the reproductive cycle in motion. A seed produces after its kind. Words are similar to seeds, and their reproductive powers are far-reaching.

Reflection

- What have been your major insights regarding the words in your internal and external conversations?
- Opportunity: You have the power to choose. Start by planting seeds today that could make the most difference in your life and the lives of others.
- Knowing the possible far-reaching positive impact of your words, what bold first steps might you choose to ensure more positive words in your conversations?

Notes

Chapter 4

Choices and Spin-Off Benefits

> Always bear in mind that your own resolution to succeed is more important than any other one thing.
>
> —Abraham Lincoln

AN INITIAL STEP TO REACH your destiny is to make a choice. Although it may appear to be obvious and overly simplistic, it is fundamental to your transformation. Even if you decide to do nothing, you have made a choice. You have the freedom to choose.

Quantity and Quality of Words

When a baby is growing and attempting to learn words, he or she is like a sponge absorbing so much. After hearing millions of words during the first three years of life, a baby starts choosing and stringing words together to speak. During the first months after birth, however, the baby is keenly attentive to the voices and faces as people talk. To learn a language, the baby has to know lots of words.

University of Kansas researchers Betty Hart and Todd R. Risley conducted a two-and-a-half-year study in the 1960s of forty-two families comprising thirteen high socioeconomic status (SES) families, ten middle SES families, and thirteen low SES families.[1] Along with their families, the researchers observed these children from seven months old until they were three years old. Results indicated that the number of words to which the children were exposed correlated to their families' status: children from low SES families heard about 616 words per hour compared to those from the higher SES families—1,251 words per hour and 2,153 words per hour. The researchers concluded that the children from the high SES families were exposed to thirty million more words than the low SES families over the duration of the study. This was, however, not the only startling outcome of the study.

The most startling outcome of the study, in my view, was that the higher SES families' words were more positive (words of praise, encouragement, etc.) than the low SES families. This is particularly important since the study revealed that 86–98 percent of the children's vocabulary came from their parents. Consider the impact of the multiplier effect and words producing after themselves.

Choose to Create Your Wonderful World

You reap what you plant inside your mind and soul. If you plant papaya seeds, you will eventually get papaya plants—not pepper plants! The soil does not decide the kind of plant that is produced. This is a critical point. Once the words take root and the germination process starts, the type of plant or fruit that results is a fait accompli.

The past is important to help you better understand yourself and determine your current state of affairs. The past cannot be changed. The future can be changed by transforming your thoughts and words. As you start or continue on your journey of transformation, be attentive to the words spoken around and inside you.

I hope you are starting to get a glimpse of the commanding force of words and that you can choose to use this force positively and in a wholesome way for your benefit and those in your world.

Proactively choose to

- attach positive and productive meanings to your words,
- remove contaminants from your sounds/words,
- cultivate the soil of your heart, and
- have a say in your future.

Choose to become truly remarkable and a wonder of your world—a wonder of the world.

Wonder, Appreciation, and Reflection

Recap

The quantity and quality of words absorbed and spoken early in our lives serve an important vocabulary foundation. You have the power to choose to add, eliminate, and redefine words and meanings for your benefit.

Reflection

- Reflect on a season in your life when you made a choice to change direction and resulted in immense fulfillment and benefits. What motivated you to decide in this way?
- We all make choices daily. Buck the status quo and resolve to frequently and proactively choose with purpose.

Notes

Part 2

Wake Up and Take Action

Chapter 5

Three Sides to
Every Story

Plant the seed of desire in your mind and it forms a nucleus
with power to attract to itself everything needed for its
fulfillment.

—Robert Collier

THE GREAT PYRAMID OF GIZA is the biggest of the three
pyramids in Giza's pyramid complex. Inside the Great
Pyramid, there are three known chambers. The pyramid
actually has four triangular sides. The other side of the story
that is not well known is that the pyramid is missing the top or
apex stone. Therefore, it was not really finished!

The Power of Three

Although the Great Pyramid of Giza has four sides, there is something fascinating about it being in a grouping of three: the sides were triangles, which are the most stable and durable of the shapes. The aura of the number three has been intriguing for thousands of years and has been pervasive in cultures and diverse areas. Many theories have surfaced to support this mysterious power of three, including the fact that three is the smallest number that forms a pattern, its size makes it easy to remember, and it represents unity of the one and two that precede it.

Unity, Rank, and Positions

o   Father, Son, Holy Spirit
o   gold, silver, bronze medals
o   beginning, middle, end

Time and Actions

o   past, present, future
o   I came, I saw, I conquered.
o   In extreme conditions, humans cannot survive more than three minutes without air, three days without water, and three weeks without food.

Words, Ideas, and Stories

o   the truth, the whole truth, and nothing but the truth
o   government of the people, by the people, for the people
o   three little pigs, three blind mice, and three musketeers

The power of three tends to facilitate the comprehension of complex concepts. I will return to the triangles in the pyramid to explain the underlying power you can create with the meanings of your words.

Triangulate to Create Meanings

Linguists C. M. Ogden and I. A. Richards explained the concept of the power of words in *The Meaning of Meaning* via a semantic triangle comprising a symbol or word (bottom left corner), a thought or reference (top), and a referent (bottom right corner).[1] The triangle conveys that the meaning of words or symbols come from within individuals. In other words, the words in and of themselves have no meaning; individuals associate their own meanings to the words. This signifies that you can create your reality with the right thoughts, mental images, or ideas appended to your words.

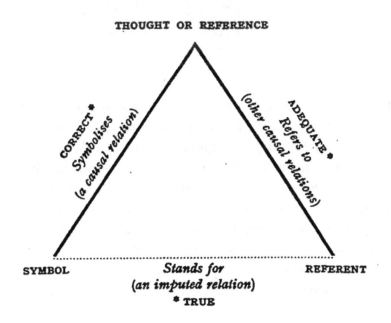

THOUGHT OR REFERENCE

CORRECT *
Symbolises
(a causal relation)

ADEQUATE *
Refers to
(other causal relations)

SYMBOL — *Stands for (an imputed relation)* — REFERENT

* TRUE

Ogden Triangle of Reference (Semantic Triangle). Figure taken from page 11, *The Meaning of Meaning* subtitled *A Study of the Influence of Language upon Thought and of the Science of Symbolism.*

To help us better appreciate Ogden's concept, let us compare it with the input-process-output framework. The symbol, sound, or word would be the input that exists prior to any connection to your thoughts or other internal references. The output is the end result of the connection to and interaction with your thoughts or other internal references.

Input-Process-Output Framework

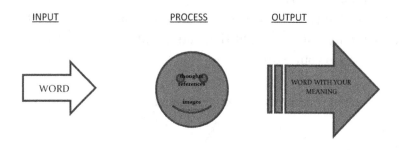

INPUT   PROCESS   OUTPUT

If you pour something into a vessel, the output depends on the contents inside the vessel. If you pour water in a vessel containing lemon juice and sugar, your output will be sweetened lemonade. You might assure me that if the vessel is absolutely clean, when water is poured in then water must come out. But if the vessel is hot enough, steam could come out; if it is cold enough, ice could come out. The output in the latter cases depends on the contents and conditions inside the vessel. An exception occurs only in supernatural circumstances: the water poured into the clay pots turned to wine because the Creator of the universe was involved.

You Are the Vessel

In the "kingdom" of words, empty vessels do not make the most noise or sound. In the context of this input-process-output framework, visualize words as seeds; void of their embryonic plants, they are meaningless. When you, the vessel, receive words and process them, the outputs are meanings. The process that transforms your words can take a while or happen in a split second. Your own words are essentially framed by what's inside. The value is generated by what is on the inside of the word. Let me further illustrate this with an observation. Some of you change the pictures within the frames in your homes or places of work from time to time. Somehow the changes give your wall or desktop a new look. While the frame or boundary surrounds the photo and perhaps adds value, the display contents within the frame are most important.

Which is more important: the *Mona Lisa* or its frame? According to the *Guinness Book of Records*, the *Mona Lisa* has received the "highest known insurance valuation for a painting," in December 1962 of $100 million.[2] Allowing for inflation, this value would be estimated at $794 million in 2015 dollars. Your mind is more vital than your physical body. Please do not misunderstand me. The frame has its purpose; without the frame, your house would likely crumble!

It is not uncommon for people to be so annoyed at their circumstances that they miss the essence of their true value and potential.

As I wrap up this chapter, let me make clear that, as the vessel, you can reach your full potential and skyrocket your intrinsic values. Here are three ways to do this and create meaningful progress:

- *Mind your thoughts and beliefs.* The manifestation of your hopes and dreams to reality has its genesis in your thoughts and beliefs—and not your surroundings or frames. Your behaviors and words come from your habitual thoughts and points of references. The average person has between an estimated fifty thousand and seventy thousand thoughts per day, according to Bruce Davis, and he indicated that they could quickly become overpowering at times.[3] Evaluate your thoughts and tame them—you have the power to do this. Retain only beneficial thoughts.

- *Take charge.* The coat or shield is a symbol of strength and protection. You have the strength to intercept and block meanings that will not improve your productivity. You are in charge of your actions and reactions.

Enhance your focus. Rather than focusing on what's happening around you and to you, see changes or challenges as opportunities and focus on what's ahead. Focus on your ability to implant and choose uplifting meanings to attach to the words you hear and see.

Wonder, Appreciation, and Reflection

Recap

Words like seeds have reproductive or creative power, and you as an individual have the power to associate your very own meanings to words you hear and speak. Your thoughts and internal references heavily influence the meanings you attach to words and need to be tamed. The input-process-output model and semantic triangle both suggest that you play an indispensable role in the interpretation of words.

Reflection

- You have the power to imagine, dream, and make words come to life with the meanings you create.
- In your mind's eye, see words as a key to open your soul, spirit, and body. See words as a pathway for you to become a more productively creative person.
- Reflect on how good you felt when you brought an idea to life; an example is the exhilaration, joy, and fulfillment you experience. There is more where that came from. Imagine breathing life into your words: redefine them and rewrite the rules for them. Imagine these very words bringing your dreams to life.

Notes

Chapter 6
Be the Change You Wish

Be the change you wish to see in the world.
—Mohandas Gandhi

WHEN YOU START OUT ON a journey to a new place, you might review the map to your destination beforehand and take note of certain landmarks and cross streets. Some of you have more or less absolute confidence in your global positioning systems (GPS) and might not be as concerned with checking out the route to your destination in advance. Unfamiliarity with the route makes the initial trip seem longer, but after a few times, you travel easily—without taxing your brain as much. This pattern is also seen when you embark on new trips in your life. It might seem longer and harder at first, but with repetition, it becomes easier and more spontaneous. Your wondrous transformation will likely be similar at the outset, and I encourage you to persist and achieve mastery of these growth concepts.

Dormancy Does Not Equal Latency

There are many words that have absolutely no impact on you because you are not aware of them or have not attached any meaning to them. In other words, the words are either hidden (latent) or asleep (dormant) according to their Latin roots *latere* and *dormire.*

Powerless without a Power Source

Words remain asleep and powerless until you attach meanings to them. Without the addition of meaning, they are only basic units of speech or language.

The point that follows is extremely vital: *You* have the power to create "embryonic plants" on the inside of words. The significance of this is that you ultimately create the meanings of words; the meanings come from within you.

Once empowered and grounded, these words start growing. Then, the fruits or results will be predictable.

Ground Zero

What came first: the fruit or the seed? The answer may not be as important because you cannot change the past. Instead, start at ground zero and focus on now and the future. We know that the seed is the starting point for the next generation of trees and fruits. Similarly, the meanings you attach to words can be the starting points for increased productivity.

Seed/Word-Meaning Formation

In seed plants, a male cell unites with a female cell to form a fertilized egg that divides to form a plant embryo. This embryo forms a protective coat around itself to become a seed. Similarly, once a sound or word unites with a thought or reference, a series of reasoning results in the formation of a meaning (referent). This reflects the semantic triangle; when symbols or words connect with thoughts or references, meanings are created.

Protective Coat

Just as the seed coat protects the plant embryo from being degraded, the will and resolve of your heart (mind) should serve to marshal and protect helpful meanings you attach to words. In essence, your heart (mind), which controls the body, should function as a gatekeeper to block and control what goes in and what goes out.

GIGO

The acronym GIGO (garbage in, garbage out) was the response when the computer was blamed for everything under the sun. The computer simply did as it was told! The heart functions in a similar way. When you repeatedly say, "I'm so unlucky" or "This good thing is not going to last," what do you expect is going to happen?

Be mindful of subtle ways words sneak into your heart. You might really like a particular style of music and gravitate to songs written in this style without paying attention to the lyrics. You then listen to the songs over and over again. Without your conscious awareness, the words become deeply rooted in your heart and sprout out in your behavior and words.

My beautiful wife loves flowers. Something about the colors brings a smile to her face, sparks feelings of joy, and puts a spring in her dance. When we first moved to Canada during the spring, she marveled at the bright yellow flowers that were ubiquitous, blanketing the public green spaces bordering the roads. Spring signifies new beginnings—and so do yellow flowers. The flowers my wife admired were dandelions; their name originates from French *Dent de lion*, meaning *lion's tooth*.

For lawn lovers, dandelions are like a prey facing its worst nightmare—the lion's teeth! Dandelions are wildflowers. The seeds of these "lively" flowers are easily spread by the wind and insects. Their taproots can grow down ten inches. The tough part is uprooting them because the taproots are delicate and break easily. Unfortunately, any part of the taproot that remains in the soil will regenerate. This is one of the reasons they are so plentiful. Undesirable words and meanings are akin to these dandelions.

In part 2, I share ways to effectively uproot undesirable words that have somehow anchored themselves in the soil of your heart.

As suggested in the introductory chapters, the practice of speaking good words into your heart can be transformational. Therefore, if you keep planting good words in the soil of your heart, good fruits will be produced. Good in, good out! GIGO!

Wonder, Appreciation, and Reflection

Recap

You are in the unique position to infuse productive power and meaning into your words to spark the changes you wish. By the same token, you have the ability to protect your helpful words and meanings from contamination. Caution is required to ensure that unproductive words and meanings do not sneak into your mind and spirit and take firm root.

Reflection

- Sleeping giants evoke images of well-rested hulk-like powers who are waiting to be awakened. Words, once the meanings have been created, are like sleeping giants.
- In your heart, you have the responsibility to ensure that they get quality sleep so that—when they are awakened—they can be refreshing, energetic, and supportive of your productivity.
- What could make the most difference going forward in the way you protect your lexicon of meaningful words from being disrupted and overtaken by undesirable words?

Notes

Chapter 7

Harness Your Power

Be still, absolutely still!
—Jesus

O F THE ESTIMATED 650 SKELETAL muscles of the human body, which do you think would be the toughest to harness? Some might conclude that it has to be gluteus maximus because it is the largest muscle and is integral in supporting the trunk of the body, the upper leg, and pelvis. Others may say that it must be the muscles that control the blinking since they support about 100,000 blinks daily. However, as many of you know, the busiest is not always the strongest. So then, it has to be the heart, right? It pumps 9,450 liters (2,500 gallons) of blood every day. It is definitely the hardest-working muscle.

For sure, it must be the masseter muscle: the one in the cheek and at the back of the jaw. Its task is to open and close the

45

jaw. Those of you who have been bitten by a toddler have a full appreciation of the force generated by this muscle.

The toughest muscle or group of muscles to harness is none of the above, in my opinion. The one I am thinking of works all the time, really, even when you are asleep, and it is tenacious. It is active in precision tasks, and it can bend, cup, and contort itself.

Physically and figuratively, in my opinion, the tongue is the toughest to harness despite the tether holding it down in the front and it being anchored into the hyoid bone at the back of the mouth. It is mobile and can move in almost all directions. It is actively involved in tasting (with thousands of taste buds), chewing, swallowing, talking, and singing. It does not take a lot of effort to use this instrument of speech, which explains its high activity (as previously mentioned about sixteen thousand spoken words per day). More importantly, given its connection to the heart and its role in expressing the contents of the heart, it is referred to as a mirror of the heart. The latter suggests that the tongue has inexpressible power, which is often difficult to control.

The word *harness* might trigger images of an animal being controlled, an individual being strapped to an anchor to prevent a perilous fall, or an entity making use of natural resources to generate energy. Given that words have constructive and destructive powers, you benefit when you control and restrain them. You also have the ability to experience positive growth when you use words to generate energy to enhance your value.

Safety Harness

I watched an astounding event unfold on television. My breathing was tight, and my heart pounded a bit faster than usual for twenty-two minutes. I wanted to close my eyes after seeing the impressive views from the cameras showing a man holding on for dear life 1,500 feet (457 meters) above a river near the Grand Canyon (a UNESCO World Heritage Site). The gusty winds exceeded thirty miles per hour (forty-eight kilometers per hour). This must have added to the unimaginable stress the man's wife and children experienced as they watched. The man's great-grandfather fell to his death under eerily similar circumstances. Was history about to repeat itself?

I had witnessed thirty-four-year Nik Wallenda, a tightrope walker, crossing a quarter-mile stretch over the Little Colorado River on a two-inch-thick (five-centimeter) steel cable—without a safety harness! The Discovery Channel arranged for Wallenda to have a microphone and two cameras attached to give the thirteen million live television viewers a realistic sense of what he was experiencing. He was walking at the equivalent height of a 138-story building. The winds were stronger than he had anticipated, which caused the tightrope to sway. He was faced with the antithetical reality of literally having to maintain his physical and mental balance. Physically, he had to use the balance pole that he held cautiously with both hands. Then something happened that perplexed me. I thought, *Oh no! What in the world is he doing?* He hesitated and crouched on the high wire. He regained composure and continued; mentally, it appeared as though he took the position that there was no turning back.

During the walk, he started talking. He was calmly speaking words of gratitude, respect, and instructions (telling the winds to go away!).[1] As he neared the other side of the gorge, he paused again! This time, he knelt on the high wire, blew a kiss, got up again, jogged to the finish, and kissed the ground when he arrived.

His spoken words, along with his training and beliefs, became his safety net. His words propelled him safely to his destination on the other side. When you speak words, every part of your body hears your voice and responds accordingly. Choose your words carefully. The intensity of your response to your words can create such propulsion that you defy the odds and successfully reach the finish lines set by your heart.

At times, you might feel like you are walking on a tightrope with strong headwinds and no harness. Take a lesson from Wallenda: pause, crouch, and be still from time to time. A *Sky News* report provided his reason for crouching was to "get the rhythm out of the rope."[2] Therefore, make use of your positive words by speaking to steady yourself safely toward your destination.

This worked so well for Wallenda that he pushed himself further in 2014 and performed tightrope walks in Chicago. The result was two new entries in the *Guinness Book of World Records*, including one for the highest blindfolded tightrope walk.

Words in Shining Armor

Knights in shining armor provide assistance to others in times of dire need. For many of you, images of chivalrous persons come to mind. But what about the shining armor itself? It does not get as much attention despite the fact that it is brilliant, gleaming, and conspicuously fine! It keeps the famous knights safe by shielding their bodies.

Harnesses are often viewed as providing control and preventing falls. They are less frequently viewed as protecting the body from attack. Harnesses can also serve as armor. According to the *Collins Dictionary*, a harness is an "armor collectively," and the transitive verb form is "to equip or clothe with armor."[3] Your words are also armor for the protection of your mind, body, and spirit.

How are words like armor?

- *They identify you.* They allow you to be recognized as a part of a particular group. They provide the protection of the group. This social grouping is sometimes called a herd, and the word *herd* has a lot in common with a harness. A herd (the person) controls, protects, and cares for others. A herd (the group) pulls together to benefit from communal strength against predators. The collection of positive words you speak has the power to ward off the predators that seek to kill your dreams. Let positive words blazon across your armor to create an unmistakable identity.

- *They prepare you for and protect you in battle.* When a well-trained soldier goes out to battle on the frontlines, he or she is amply prepared, armed, and armored. Words can build confidence, train you to be emotionally and mentally fit, instill discipline, and inspire resiliency. In life, use your words to win your battles.

- *They provide you with a refuge.* When you read, meditate on, and speak words of value such that they are planted deep within you, you create a safe haven for your retreat. In this place, you are sheltered and out of harm's way.

Harness Your Words

Words have life. As such, they are comprised of units that have the potential to grow and reproduce. Their meanings change, depending on context and audience. Words get, give, and use energy. One of the startling properties of energy that seemed, irreconcilable from my early school education, is that energy cannot be created or destroyed. Energy, however, can be transferred when forces interact.

From many examples, including Wallenda's tightrope experience, it is apparent that the kinetic energy contained in spoken words has tremendous power. And since the power is not destroyed, how can you make use of your words to transfer this power and redeploy it to constructively change your world? What if the energy from the approximately sixteen thousand words spoken daily could be harnessed? Imagine the multiplier effect.

The upcoming chapters unveil the powerful potential of harnessing your words for your benefit.

Wonder, Appreciation, and Reflection

Recap

The tongue is considered one of the most difficult parts of the body to effectively harness. The power of your words spoken and facilitated by the tongue reverberates throughout your body and has the ability to unite and protect your mind, body, and spirit. The energy generated by words can be used productively to trigger achievement of your wishes.

Reflection

- Harnesses require connection. Words come alive when they are connected to meanings.
- In the early 1960s, a worldwide connection of computers was envisioned, and shortly thereafter, the Internet was conceived. The Internet, like words, has the power to be constructive and destructive.
- Select a personal high point in your life that resulted from self-talk or words you meditated upon. Now choose a dream or desire that you have put on the back burner and imagine at least three constructive ways you could bring it to the forefront.

Notes

Chapter 8
Choose to Be a Friend of Your Destiny

If fear is cultivated it will become stronger, if faith is cultivated it will achieve mastery.

—John Paul Jones

WORDS HAVE LIFE. YOUR WORDS will yield productive fruits when they are conceived and nurtured in a friendly setting. One of the wisest men who walked the face of this earth, King Solomon, revealed this principle when he aptly said, "As iron sharpens iron, so a friend sharpens a friend."[1] This comparison cogently suggests that a friend cultivates growth to make others better in all ways. Such friends engender faith. Faith is characterized by confidence, fidelity, and trust—often when there is no proof. This is the reason some of you fly in airplanes without validating the training of the pilot or the fact that the person flying the airplane is indeed a pilot! Civil rights leader Dr. Martin Luther King Jr. fittingly described this confidence: "Faith is taking the first step, even when you don't see the whole staircase."[2] Faith is a friend to your words and your destiny.

Fear, on the other hand, has the capacity to precipitate a chain of negative thoughts into counterproductive words that eventually lead to unproductive actions. Oftentimes, fear has the ability to paralyze actions and decisions. These unpleasant feelings about what will happen need to be harnessed and minimized. The fear factor is a foe to your destiny, and it keeps you away with diversions and roadblocks.

I will share a spy story to demonstrate how friendly words have the ability to open amazing doors of opportunity and how fearful words can destroy the paths to your destiny. This particular spy story demonstrates the contrasting impact of faith and fear. This particular story brought to life the saying "what you *see* is what you get."

Notice that information gathered from spying is frequently called intelligence (it does have a more agreeable ring than Central Spying Agency, the spying community, and Secret Spying Service).

Gathering Intelligence

Twelve leaders were selected to be spies and were given a mandate to go in and observe a country that had been targeted for takeover. They were asked to complete a SWOT analysis (strengths, weaknesses, opportunities, and threats) of the people, land, security, living environment, and agriculture. Lastly, they were encouraged to bring back samples of the fruits from the country given its reputation as a fertile land.[3]

Their intelligence-gathering trip lasted forty days.

Ten of the leaders presented a dismal report, and two of the leaders presented a positive report. Permit me to segment the spies into two groups based on how they presented their reports to the other leaders and people at the end of the mission: 80 percent leaders (ten leaders with dismal report) and 20 percent leaders (two leaders with positive report).

80 Percent Leaders (10 Leaders)—Country Intelligence Report, Highlights

- People: strong
- Security: fortified
- Land: very large
- Agriculture: lots of milk, honey

This was a summary of a lopsided analysis that used good words and focused explicitly on the strengths and implicitly on the threats of the country. In other words, there were no weaknesses or opportunities. Despite a clearly lucrative country, the 80 percent leaders were petrified as a result of their mission, which clouded their report and sowed seeds of fear in the people. These 80 percent leaders used the fear factor.

Their recommendation: "We are not able to go up against the people for they are too strong for us."

After receiving the report, the seeds of fear instilled by the 80 percent leaders caused the people to weep aloud and cry throughout the night. Since seeds produce after themselves, let us take a look at this in play (figures 1 and 2) with these people.

Figure 1

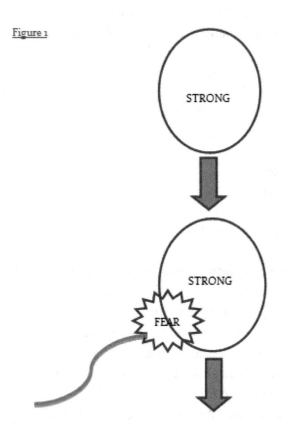

WORD (SEED) CREATED: THEIR MEANING OF STRONG

<u>Figure 2</u>

FRUIT: RESULTS

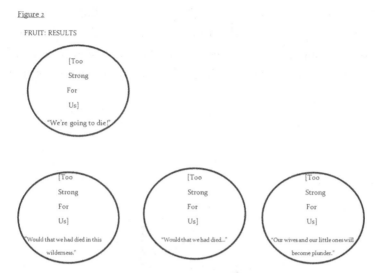

The fear absorbed by the 80 percent leaders actually poisoned their spoken words that were sowed and yielded a miserable future for these people. The people grumbled and complained incessantly to the annoyance of the leaders. In fact, the people were so frustrated at the optimism of the 20 percent leaders that they petitioned to have them stoned! History records that the 80 percent leaders and the people who followed them were essentially in a holding pattern for forty years. Sadly, they died in the wilderness without traveling to the lucrative spied-out country. Unfortunately, what they *said* was what they got.

Fear is one of the biggest foes that can taint your words and stop you from pursuing your dreams. Learn to recognize fear. Sometimes it is cloaked as reality and honesty, but never give in to it. Instead, choose the path of faith.

20 Percent Leaders (2 Leaders)—Intelligence Report Recap

While the two leaders of the group agreed entirely with the descriptive words shared by the 80 percent leaders, their disposition was completely different. One of them saw endless opportunities and was not frightened by the illusions of fear. His words were filled with confidence. "We should by all means go up and take possession of it, for we will surely overcome it."

Figures 3 and 4 show the impact of this confident disposition.

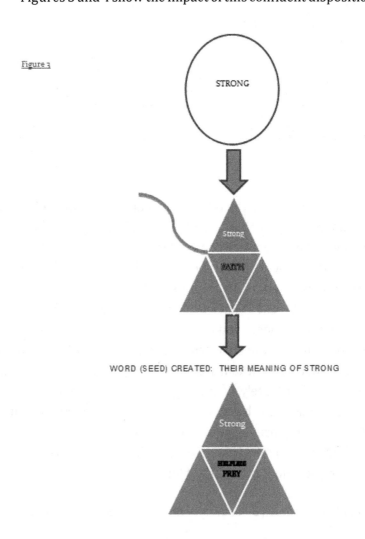

Figure 3

STRONG

Strong

FAITH

WORD (SEED) CREATED: THEIR MEANING OF STRONG

Strong

HELPLESS
PREY

FRUIT: RESULTS

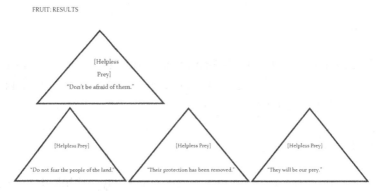

Faith actually inspired boldness in the words spoken by the 20 percent leaders, and it ultimately yielded victory. History records that the 20 percent leaders were successful in reaching the spied-out country. They had so much faith that they tenaciously held on to the possibilities of victory. They were inspired by what they saw in the spied-out country. What they *said* was what they got: triumphant possession of the lucrative country!

Practice embracing thoughts of confidence and faith. This will create an environment conducive to meaningful words and actions that are resolutely faithful to your destiny.

Wonder, Appreciation, and Reflection

Recap

Words have life and can determine the course of your life. Faith or fear will influence the meanings associated with your words. Faith cultivates; fear destroys.

Reflection

- You exercise your faith every single day—think about it. Examples include when you turn on your stove, put your key in the ignition, or sit on a chair. You have no scientific proof each time that your stove will come on, your car will start, or your chair will not collapse, but you take the first step of faith.
- You have actually exhibited such faith with many things and in many areas of your life you consider mundane.
- Allow this faith to seed and permeate your thinking. Imagine yourself as a sponge. Dive into the water of faith—and absorb every hopeful ounce of it. This will strengthen your base, unleash new possibilities, and take you from strength to strength like iron sharpening iron.

Notes

_____

_____

_____

_____

_____

_____

_____

_____

_____

_____

_____

_____

_____

_____

_____

_____

_____

_____

_____

_____

_____

_____

_____

_____

_____

_____

_____

_____

_____

_____

Chapter 9
Infuse Power in Your Words

There are incalculable resources in the human spirit, once it has been set free.

—Hubert H. Humphrey

Get Out of the Rut and Into the Groove

DAY IN AND DAY OUT, you do the same old, same old. Over and over, you routinely travel your paths, and then one day, you realize that you are in a rut. You are stuck! You want to get out.

With much excitement, a girl told her dad that his tie was "on fleek." Because of his confused expression, she explained that his tie was fabulous, made him look quite fashionable, and was on point. In thanking her, he shared with her that, in his heyday, her mom often complimented him for his "groovy" ties. It's interesting how word meanings fade, emerge, and evolve over time.

The expression "getting in the groove" relates to performing well and is believed to have its roots in the functioning of record players. When the needle of the record player was in the groove or very fine spiral cut of the vinyl record, recorded sounds emerged from the audio speakers.

For you to reach your full potential, you need to be *willing* to move forward. Unfortunately, some people get stuck in the groove and struggle to figure out how to get out. One of the key ways to get breakthroughs and consistently hit your stride is to have a *willing* attitude. While this may seem very basic, countless successful people have attested that this has been an important ingredient in their secret sauce. So why don't more people view life and various pursuits through this lens? It may be closely tied to the differences between being *willing* and being willful.

Being *willing* suggests a noticeable happiness or readiness to do something. In my opinion, this attitude, outlook, or approach connects you well within the groove, builds bridges, and is positive.

Being *willful* suggests a tenacious hold on a position or view despite clarification or reasonable explanations. In my view, this outlook or approach disconnects from the groove, burns bridges, and is negative.

Groove Alignments

For legitimate reasons, you may no longer want to do what you're doing or be where you are. Be *willing* to adjust your outlook, and be courageous enough to change course and do something else or be somewhere else.

Have a willing attitude. This is an important success factor for you to internalize. From time to time, we all need to have "will adjustments." You take your cars for wheel adjustments to decrease the wear and tear on your tires. When a car's wheels are out of alignment, it will drift to the left or right. If not corrected, the tires will wear out quickly.

Some of you might feel off-center or like you are wearing yourself out. Consider a *will* adjustment. This could mean "rotating your tires" or changing the way you do or see things. It could also mean "realigning your tires" or lining up your thoughts, words, attitudes, and actions in the same direction.

Breaking Records

Sometimes you shortchange yourself from reaching your full potential because you do not believe that you are good enough, old enough, smart enough, or healthy enough. I watched a news recap of a World Cup soccer game between the United States and Belgium, and I could not help but reflect on how exceptional performances can occur even in difficult situations.[1] Although the United States lost the game, goalkeeper Timothy Howard had a record-breaking sixteen saves during the game.

When Tim Howard was in the sixth grade, he was diagnosed with Tourette's syndrome (a movement disorder with physical and vocal tics, sudden movements like eye blinking or twitching, and involuntary muscle movements). His mother spoke good words to him, frequently declaring that he could do anything he put in his mind. These words yielded positive fruits, and the words planted in his 1997 high school yearbook below his picture show the multiplier effect in play: "It will take a nation of millions to hold me back." In 2012, he became only the fourth goalkeeper in the English Premier League to score a goal. According to a 2014 CNN news story, US National team coach Jurgen Klinsmann indicated that Howard was one of the top five goalkeepers in the world.[2]

What would happen if you adopted Howard's belief and determination? You are worth so much and should commit to speaking words that infuse you with an unstoppable drive to reach your full potential.

Beating the Odds

As a young boy, I would walk past my neighbor's home and observe the "childlike" paintings on his boundary wall, not thinking they were anything special. Some neighbors thought the paintings were too childishly simplistic and thought the home owner—a professional housepainter—should have known better. In a news article reporting on the artist's death in 2009, the *New York Times* quoted him as saying, "Used to be, I could count the people in the Bahamas who understood my work."[3]

This very humble man, one of fourteen children, left his birthplace of the Exumas in the Bahamas to seek employment in New Providence, the capital. Amos Ferguson was born in 1920 and only started showing his artistic work in the Bahamas in the early 1970s.

He did not lament his background of being a housepainter with very little schooling from a very small community. He had the ability to see what others struggled to see; when the local community rejected his paintings as he displayed them for sale, he was not overly discouraged. He saw the potential of his work and said, "I paint by faith, not by sight."

His words liberated him and charted a wonderful future. Galerie Bonheur in Saint Louis saw the value of his work and sold his paintings. By the late 1970s, an American collector purchased several of his pieces and showed them to an art dealer. The collector and dealer returned to Nassau with a view of getting a museum to purchase more paintings. His words liberated him and charted a wonderful future.

- The street where he resided was posthumously renamed Amos Ferguson Street.
- One of the oldest public museums in the United States, Wadsworth Atheneum Museum of Art, featured his pieces on March 31, 1985.
- In 1990, Ferguson was awarded the Order of the British Empire by Queen Elizabeth II.

According to the official blog of the National Art Gallery of the Bahamas, "He is considered one of the pioneers of Bahamian art and was one of the first artists to put the Bahamas on the map."[4]

Regardless of your circumstances, you have what it takes to reach your full potential. Get firmly connected to this principle— and create memorable milestones on your journey.

Let Go of the Bird in Hand

The title of this section might appear to be irresponsible advice: "A bird in the hand is worth two in the bush." This proverb suggests that it is better to hold on to what you have than to let it go at the risk of not having anything at all. While I do not fully disagree with the spirit of this proverb, I believe it is sometimes an overused reason for not acting, which impedes personal and professional growth. When a plane is in a holding pattern, it is waiting for permission and going "nowhere fast." In other words, it may be close to its destination, but in order to get there, the pilot has to get out of the pattern and safely land.

I have read several versions of a folk story regarding the monkey who lost its freedom because it held on too long. It was not prepared to give up something it thought was valuable.

The story conveys that a hunter had set a trap for the monkey. He placed a banana in a cage built with vertical bars spaced to permit the monkey's open hand to fit through the bars but not wide enough for its fist. The cage was bolted to the ground to prevent the monkey from dragging it. Once the monkey got its hand through the bars and clutched the banana, it tried many ways to get the banana out without success. It kept holding on to the banana and thinking, *I'm so close*. It did not realize it was a trap. The hunter came along and captured the monkey. The monkey was so close to freedom—all it had to do was let go!

For many of you, your breakthroughs are so close. When you let go, wonders will occur. Once you let go, you begin to understand how it liberates you to make progress, experience fulfillment, and achieve new discoveries.

Wonder, Appreciation, and Reflection

Recap

Your words are infused with seminal power when you have a willing attitude. From time to time, you will benefit from having "will alignments" to ensure that your attitudes, thoughts, and words are in sync. Words can liberate or entrap.

Reflection

- "Letting go" has been the tipping point of success for countless individuals.
- According to the *Guinness Book of World Records*, 321,197 dominoes were toppled sequentially with just one tip by Liu Yang on December 31, 2011.[5]
- To make the most meaningful difference, how can you adapt your beliefs and use your words to push the first domino, which could pave the way to your vision of the future?

Notes

Chapter 10

Treat Yourself to a Makeover

Although the life of a person is in a land full of thorns and weeds, there is always a space in which the good seed can grow.

—Pope Francis

YOU MIGHT TELL ME I'M a little too late with these concepts because you already know and understand (have already attached meanings to) at least forty thousand words! Although you might have a well-developed lexicon, your brain has an unquantifiable capacity to unlearn old things and learn new things.

Word Treatment—The Basics

With words, a mind-set of amenability facilitates change, creativity, and growth. This means you should be willing to embrace teachable principles to spur positive growth. Yes, this will require a measure of patience and humility. This amenability prepares you to get outside of your comfort zone and remove barriers from words. Barriers block growth. What is the impact of removing the barriers? Removing them leads to freedom and delivers a clean slate so that you can introduce fruitful meanings.

One of the family homes we purchased was about ten years old. The home was in a pretty good state of repair and the basement was newly outfitted, but the air-duct system had never been cleaned. With more than thirty vents, we expected that a proper cleaning would result in an expense we had not included in our budget. We considered the accumulation of dust, debris, possible mold and bacteria, and all the tainted air being redistributed when the heating and cooling system was activated. It was an easy decision. We did not want harmful airborne particles circulating for our constant inhalation. Without delay, we had the duct system cleaned and disinfected to kill any bacteria or mold, thereby restoring an acceptable standard of air quality in the house. The filter was also replaced to continue to protect the mechanical parts of the system from particles and debris.

While you may be attractive and in pretty good physical shape, your words might not be as desirable. It is similar to the unhealthy accumulations in our home's duct system. To free your heart from harmful words and thoughts circulating in your consciousness, you need to resolutely take restorative steps.

Self-reflect. It is important to take stock and take a true internal look at your nature, your purpose, your beliefs, your outlook on life, and your attitude toward yourself. Ponder your traits, thoughts, and conversations with others and yourself. What words and phrases come up frequently? Why do you opt to use certain words? Are they mostly positive, neutral, or negative? Bear in mind that many of your linguistic habits are unconscious. Pay close attention, make notes, and journal about your observations.

Look over your shoulder. By looking over your shoulders, I am not suggesting that you watch your back! Despite your thorough self-introspection, there may be conversational tendencies that you are not aware of. The best way to identify these blind spots is to take an extra look over your shoulder and seek trusted feedback from someone who knows you well. Ask for a candid assessment of your words. Are they mostly positive, neutral, or negative?

Act. Armed with this insightful information from your self-reflection and feedback from others, it is time to take responsibility for the word quality in your heart. Stephen Covey aptly captured this notion when he wrote, "To learn and not to do is really not to learn. To know and not to do is really not to know."

Heart Treatment—The Basics

When I make references to your heart, I am referring to your soul, your mind, and your core. My recommendation of self-reflection in the preceding section was intended to encourage you to explore your very own experiences throughout your body—not just in your brain or heart. Your heart impacts your survival and is similar to soil that keeps mineral nutrients close to the roots that have sprouted outside of the seed. Your heart feeds and provides nourishment to the meaning of words. In order for your heart to function effectively in this way, helpful nutrients must be present. What is the best way for them to get in your heart? They get there through your proactivity. Take control and take advance steps to influence your destiny.

Your primary line of defense is to attach lots of positive and constructive meanings to words you encounter and speak. This will form the basis of a healthy mind-set and will crowd out negative thoughts and speaking. Research has demonstrated that the brain has a bias toward negative information and negative information is more impactful than equally positive information. Dr. John T. Cacioppo, a distinguished professor at the University of Chicago, and other researchers concluded that the brain has greater sensitivity to bad news. You might now understand how "bad news travels faster."[1]

Step out and begin your journey of getting rid of all of those unhelpful thoughts, perceptions, and paradigms that influence the meanings you attach to words. You will need to be very mindful that getting rid of these unhelpful references could come with complicated emotions. Be courageous and fully appreciate that this process is not a one-shot deal. This is a renewal that requires your commitment for the long haul. Remind yourself frequently about why you are eliminating these unhelpful traits and the benefits that can multiply for you and others.

Let go and declutter your hearts of these unhelpful traits.

Word Treatment—Makeover

Babies listen and observe intently before they start speaking in simple babbles. Now that you have listened and observed your word traits, start small. Look for easy traits to add and eliminate. For example, start talking to yourself positively. Instead of saying, "I'll never get back in shape," say, "The strong love I have for my body will motivate me to stick to my exercise routines." Researchers, including Dr. Cacioppo, have discovered that small positive experiences tend to have more impact on your brain than infrequent large positive experiences.[2] To counter the negativity balance in the brain, Dr. Cacioppo suggested positive inputs at the rate of "five small positives to one negative."

Stop reading, watching, and listening to worthless material. What goes in is what is going to come out (remember the GIGO principle). Start genuinely complimenting others on a daily basis and frequently express gratitude. Keep moving forward, pick up momentum, and reward yourself.

Relax more (it is okay to smile, laugh, and have fun) and refuse to hold on to retributions. Refuse to hold on to destructive attitudes, negative thinking, and selfish preoccupations. Let others off the hook to ensure that the poison of unforgiveness does not infect your heart and spill over to taint the meanings you attached to words. A poison is something destructive, something that erodes.

To get an appreciation of the harmful effect of poisons such as unforgiveness, despite their sometimes subtleness, consider the impact over time of untreated river water on tough iron and lead pipes. In places where salt is used to deice roads in winter, positive and negative chloride ions are separated as it dissolves into the water. This water contains concentrated chloride ions that overflow into the river, the source of water for some communities. The negative chloride ions are corrosive. If the river water is not treated with an anticorrosive agent, it would destroy the iron and lead pipes. Unfortunately, high levels of lead and iron would then leach into the water supply. A concentration of lead in the water supply is particularly harmful for children.

Unforgiveness is negative and becomes progressively destructive over time if it is not treated. The treatment for unforgiveness is forgiveness—repeatedly. Treat unforgiveness with words that restore relationships and heal the hearts of the forgiver and the forgiven.

"Weeds" have very little value and can block the success of the positive, productive words in your life. They grow prolifically, and if they are not rooted out, they will gain ground and take over your heart's turf. Some weeds are parasitic, and they are also known for keeping bad company and harboring undesirables like pests and diseases. Some people believe that it is acceptable to have a few weeds in their gardens, but avid gardeners know weeds are welcomed by homeless slugs! In case you think having slugs around is a good thing, consider a few of their characteristics. The majority of the slug population is underground and eats seedlings, roots, and seed sprouts! And here we go again with the multiplier effect: one slug lays between twenty and one hundred eggs several times a year, and the eggs lay dormant in the soil for years!

This is not just a battle for territorial mind space; this is a battle for the elements that keep you alive. You must thoroughly get rid of unproductive words and meanings, including their roots.

As a boy, I had the privilege (or so I was told) of removing the weeds from our flowers and other plants. For me, it was always easier to remove the young weeds. In fact, I would just pull them up by hand. The older weeds required a cutlass or pickax to ensure that all the deep roots were removed. The bigger weeds actually choked out and killed some of our flowers and plants. I now realize two things:

- Weeds fight to live just like flowers and other plants do.
- Removing weeds when they are young actually prevents a lot of backbreaking work.

Weeds are words of little value, which are a result of the unproductive and destructive meanings attached to them. Like the dandelion weed, they are prolific seed producers. One dandelion plant could produce five thousand seeds per year. Words of little value must be eliminated promptly to prevent their rapid spread.

Staying on the Offensive

As this elimination process is underway and you start regaining control, you need to step up your offensive strategy to stay ahead of the game and make sure that the weeds do not come back. This strategy involves investing in yourself. Vigorously develop your heart to be rich in positive and productive thoughts and words, which will crowd out the weeds. Sustain a healthy thought and word life by maintaining the right conditions.

Foster the right conditions in your heart with caring attitudes (temperature), bubbly and energetic temperaments (light), focused beliefs (oxygen), and positive thinking (moisture).

Wonder, Appreciation, and Reflection

Recap

A mind-set of amenability sets the foundation for change and restoration. In addition, self-reflection and responsible action will lead to sustainable results. The association of positive and constructive meanings to the words you hear and speak is a primary line of defense to adopt. Eliminate undesirable words quickly and stay on the offensive by maintaining positive and productive thoughts.

Reflection

- Throughout your life, you have faced obstacles. Think of a few of the major ones you have overcome, particularly those that you thought were impossible in the beginning.
- How are you using your ability to speak to and overcome your obstacles? Yes, you can talk to them!
- Nelson Mandela said, "It always seems impossible until it's done."

Notes

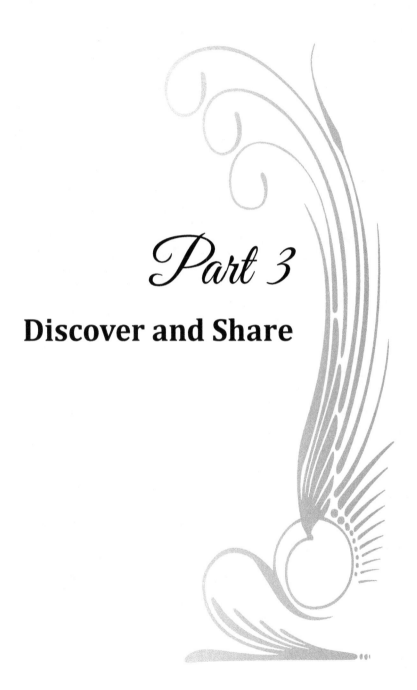

Part 3

Discover and Share

Chapter 11

Discover Your
Think Tank

The will to win, the desire to succeed, the urge to reach
your full potential ... these are the keys that will unlock
the door to personal excellence.

—Confucius

Food for Thought

WHEN THE PLANT INSIDE A seed starts to grow, it survives by absorbing its internal food; after its roots venture outside of the seed coat, it takes food from the soil. It needs food to survive. Three nutrients for plant growth come from water and air, and the other thirteen nutrients come from the soil. I previously compared the soil to the mind or heart of a human being, illustrating that most of the nutrients required for the meanings you attach to your words come from your heart. I alluded to some of these in the previous chapter and appreciate that these may vary for each individual, depending on the results you are seeking to achieve.

A Penny for Your Thoughts

What do Sir Thomas More, Mohandas Gandhi, and the apostle Paul have in common? Yes, they all have the letter a in their names. And they were all trained in the law, shared fruitful words, and highlighted the value of thoughts.

In *Four Last Things*, Sir Thomas wrote, "As so often does happen, the face itself showing the mind walking a pilgrimage, such that, not without some notice and reproach of such a vagrant mind, other folk suddenly say to one, 'A penny for your thoughts.'"[1] Sir Thomas's message was somewhat of a reprimand for a wandering mind. Therefore, it could be deduced that he intended to communicate that focused thoughts had more value.

> Keep your thoughts positive, because your thoughts become your words.
> Keep your words positive, because your words become your behavior.
> Keep your behavior positive, because your behavior becomes your habits.
> Keep your habits positive, because your habits become your values.
> Keep your values positive, because your values become your destiny.
> —Mohandas Gandhi

From prison, Paul wrote a letter to the people of the city of Philippi.[2]

And now, dear brothers and sisters, one final thing. Fix your thoughts on what is true, and honorable, and right, and pure, and lovely, and admirable. Think about things that are excellent and worthy of praise.

Nourishment for Your Soil

Gandhi's words of wisdom show how you can gain momentous mileage by being positive. By being positive, you are not putting your head in the proverbial sand. You are actually being proactive by determining the quality of your journey. According to WebMD, researchers concluded from a 2010 study that painful words could actually trigger pain sensors in the brain.[3] Researcher and professor Thomas Weiss confirmed that "these findings show that words alone are capable of activating our pain matrix." What does this mean? When you frequently talk using painful words, you make matters worse because the brain responds by increasing the degree of pain you are feeling.

On the other hand, leading positive psychology researcher Dr. Barbara Fredrickson demonstrated in *Positivity* that positivity can transform your future for the better.[4] In fact, Frederickson's findings support the view that incrementally building up positive thoughts lays the foundation for extraordinary results.

If you are generous in nourishing your heart, words could be richer in meaning and exponentially more impactful in your life. Paul essentially advocated and laid out a framework for achieving and keeping positive thoughts. I recommend this framework for nourishing your heart. You are to regularly and diligently focus your thoughts on the nutrients in the table that follows.

Nutrients	Function
truth (reality, actuality, fact)	essential for firm ethical foundation
honor (principle, nobility, respect)	essential for dignity in your life
rightness (justice, uprightness, appropriateness)	essential for equitable treatment of others according to divine and human laws
purity (cleanliness, clarity, wholesomeness)	essential for your state of mind and well-being
loveliness (endearment, pleasantness, innate beauty)	essential for affable conduct, conversation, and softening the disposition of others
admirableness (reputation, agreeableness, wonderfulness)	essential for your productivity, good name, wholesomeness, and constructiveness

Here are a few examples of focusing your thoughts as outlined in the above nutrients:

- *Truth.* You have a fulfilling life, health, a loving family you focus on with a sense of gratitude.
- *Honor.* You have high regard and respect for your parents and often think of their helpful advice to you over the years.
- *Rightness.* You have a keen appreciation for diversity and marvel at the insights from this variety.
- *Purity.* You are fascinated by the ease at which some children accept and relate to others.

- *Loveliness.* You reflect on your sense of endearment to family that gives you the benefit of the doubt when you make mistakes.
- *Admirableness.* You had a pretty fulfilling day at work, and later that evening, you reflected on how grateful your colleague was for the genuine support you provided (in spite of the fact that you were so busy). Your help resulted in a major breakthrough. Your colleague shared that this inspired her to help other team members.

Gandhi and Paul fully appreciated the concept of the seed producing after its kind. They knew that inner thoughts would inseminate and germinate like words and deeds. They knew that focus and persistence were continuous twin spans on the bridge between your current position and your destiny. They concluded that positivity and excellence are essential characteristics that unite to catalyze meaningful words into wondrous deeds.

Wonder, Appreciation, and Reflection

Recap

Thoughts are a valuable and foundational nutrient in the heart. Wandering and negative thoughts intensify pain and diminish value. On the other hand, positive and focused thoughts lead to extraordinary results.

Reflection

- Some words and meanings are like perennials, which tend to live through the seasons of the year. In winter and autumn, they appear lifeless, but their rootstocks are intact and alive.
- In your thought garden, what kind of soil are you depositing throughout the year? What do you spend most of your time thinking about? What patterns are you observing from your thoughts?
- Adopt Paul's framework to guide your thoughts and impact your future.

Notes

_____

_____

_____

_____

_____

_____

_____

_____

_____

_____

_____

_____

_____

_____

_____

_____

_____

_____

_____

_____

_____

_____

_____

_____

_____

_____

_____

_____

_____

_____

_____

_____

_____

Chapter 12

Design and Build
Your World

Do what you can, with what you have, where you are.
—Theodore Roosevelt

I N CHAPTER 8, I SHOWED the importance of making confidence the building block for your words. The word *confidence* suggests that you are acting with a degree of trust that your circumstances will come together and turn out well.

When the cells of a plant come together, a new and different creation evolves even though this might not be externally evident. When the sounds of words come together with your references or thoughts, you create meanings. The words in this book have been written to spur a difference in your perspectives and ultimately in your heart. Your words can make a difference in your destiny and your destination—from where you are now to where you would like to be.

You are the main contractor with the responsibility of designing and building your world where you would like to take up residence.

Playing Well

To play well with others implies that you interact harmoniously with others in social and work settings. As elucidated in the previous chapter, when you interlock your thoughts to positive and excellent things, your life turns out well.

After his wife died while giving birth to their fourth son, Ole Kirk Christiansen was left with the responsibility of raising four boys. In 1924, while two of his sons were playing, a fire destroyed the family's carpentry workshop and home. These unfortunate events—along with the onset of the Great Depression—did not stop this carpenter from doing what he could with what he had. He kept on making everyday household items and used the scrap wood to make toys.[1] In 1932, Christiansen established the LEGO Group in Billund, Denmark.[2] This group is one of the world's largest toy manufacturers.

LEGO is a combination of two Danish words "LEg GOdt" meaning "play well." In Latin, *lego* means "I put together." The company has claimed that its most important product is the LEGO plastic brick, and the way the company describes the principle behind this product epitomizes the spirit of my message throughout this book. Here's the description from the company's website:

> The interlocking principle with its tubes makes it unique and offers unlimited building possibilities. It's just a matter of getting the

imagination going—and letting a wealth of creative ideas emerge through play.

Design

> Ideas rose in clouds; I felt them collide until pairs interlocked, so to speak, making a stable combination.
> —Henri Poincare

With your words, you have unlimited possibilities. Let your thoughts and ideas interlock to generate uplifting words that lead manifestly to your heart's desires. Your words are like the LEGO bricks, and when they connect to images and references, you can design and literally bring your dreams to life. Consider your possibilities. Picture the future you want. Take some time to explore your hopes and dreams. When you are exploring, let yourself go without being held back by judgments, criticisms, and other people's opinions. Maintain a friendly environment of faith.

Here's a small sampling of designs that actually manifested using LEGO's interlocking plastic bricks and made it into the *Guinness Book of World Records.*

- Tower: tallest structure built as at June 21, 2015; Milan, Italy; 114 ft. 11 in. (35.05 m).[3]
- Caravan: largest camper completed for display October 13–18, 2015; Birmingham, UK; 7.2 ft. (2.2 m) tall by 11.8 ft. (3.6 m) long.[4]
- Ball Contraption: largest great ball contraption ("a machine intended to pass a ball from one location to another through a series of mechanical steps contained within modules"); December 2015; London, 100 individual modules.[5]

Building

The building process continues with you talking to yourself. You see athletes doing this frequently because they know that self-talk can enhance performance. Sports psychologist Dr. Antonis Hatzigeorgiadis shared in a news article that self-talk (mental strategy using cue words and phrases) is the connection between your thoughts and performance.[6] These cue words and phrases should be positive and in alignment with the desired performance.

This self-talk strategy of interlocking your dreams with meaningful words should be repeated on a consistent basis. Such repetition can change the environment of your thought world and establish a solid foundation that supports the building blocks of your dreams. As Dr. Hatzigeorgiadis highlighted, the primary objectives of self-talk are "to enhance your potential; and to perform during competition in terms of your ability and not less."

It is important for me to repeat what I previously shared: you get what you say.

Wonder, Appreciation, and Reflection

Recap

The responsibility of designing and building your world is in your hands. You are the principal contractor. You can generate words to open unlimited possibilities. Consistency should be practiced by engaging in self-talk to interlock your dreams with meaningful words.

Reflection

- When you are designing your dreams, you are in the driver's seat. You are making the choice about where you go. Please do not be bashful.
- With these dreams, be conscious of the world you are designing. More importantly, be conscious that you are designing a better world for you.
- From this positive perspective, and once you have a few designs ready for construction, consider how this might impact your internal and external conversations. Start building.

Notes

_____

_____

_____

_____

_____

_____

_____

_____

_____

_____

_____

_____

_____

_____

_____

_____

_____

_____

_____

_____

_____

_____

_____

_____

_____

_____

_____

_____

_____

_____

Chapter 13

Change for Better

Continuous effort—not strength or intelligence—is the
key to unlocking our potential.

—Winston Churchill

IN THE EARLY STAGES OF a plant's growth from a seed,
nutrients and the right conditions are required on a
sustained basis to promote healthy survival. Incrementally,
this plant grows stronger and continues the cycle of producing
fruit and then seeds.

Changing Winds

Change connotes becoming different. Your words can make a
difference in your destiny and your destination—from where
you are now to where you would like to be.

Change is easier if you have the will to change. The will to change is similar to the wind, which is not readily visible. However, depending on the speed of the wind, you are able to see clues regarding its direction. Sprinters in single-direction races experience this when their speed is helped while they are running in the same direction of the wind or negatively impacted while they are running in the opposite direction. If you have the will to change, it can help you move more quickly toward your goals and destinations. Conversely, if you do not have the will to change, you will most likely struggle and battle "against the winds."

You can play a proactive role in your change by being willing to change. You can have a say in the direction of your change. You can choose to change for the better.

Strength in Unity

Once you choose to change, you need to start moving. Get up and take unified action.

To move from dormancy to growth, at the very outset, the right conditions are required to spark change for the better. Once growth starts within the seed, the rate of consumption increases quickly and causes the small plant to push roots outside of the seed coat and reach out for nutrients to stay alive and continue growing. Then the plant consumes the water and nutrients from the soil—together with carbon dioxide from the air and energy from the sun—to produce its own food for strength.

When there is alignment and unity of positive thoughts and words, the sky is the limit for your achievements. To demonstrate this power, let's go back in history to 2200 BC. A group of people in Shinar only spoke one language; in fact, it was reportedly the only language spoken in the world at that time.[1] They put into words what they wanted to do and then took action in unity. They had progressive thoughts: "Let's be productive." Then they put those thoughts into words by sharing those words with others. The people suggested to one another that they should start making bricks. Their words led them to take action. They gained momentum and got really good at making bricks; in fact, they could do it without thinking too hard. It soon became a habit. Their progress gave meaning to their words and led them to develop core beliefs about working together in a unified manner.

They put these core beliefs into words and created a proposal to build a city for themselves! They did not stop at their brick-making success because they understood that words interlocked with unified core beliefs could be powerful. I wonder if these people were ancestors of the builders of the 481-foot Great Pyramid of Giza.

These people wanted to build a city, and they wanted to become well known. With this desire to become famous, their destiny was to build a tower that would far exceed the height of the Great Pyramid of Giza. Their destiny was a man-made structure that would tower over all—and its capstone would reach the skies.

This awesome aspiration and destiny started with thoughts that seeded words. These words formed the foundation for their actions, which unleashed such potential that the Creator of the universe said, "If as one people speaking the same language they have begun to do this, then *nothing* [emphasis added] they plan to do will be impossible for them."

Please be sure to read the next chapter of this book to learn more about the outcome of this magnificent project of the Shinar people.

See and Feel before You Speak

Your thoughts, desires, and words set in motion the possibilities in your life. The people of Shinar used words to paint pictures of what they were thinking. The initiators in the group were probably able to clearly visualize their desires with the eyes of their hearts.

As a child, I was taught to look left, then right, and left again before crossing the street. In fact, traffic laws required motorists to stop once I set foot onto the pedestrian crossing. This action of looking before stepping onto the crossing spoke louder than just knowing the way across the street. It is critically important to take *lead* actions when pursuing your heart's desires. Simply put, *lead* actions are taken beforehand to influence the outcomes. Therefore, looking left, right, and then left again were *lead* actions to prevent an accident when crossing the street. There is a "street" between where you are today and where you would really like to be in the future.

If you hire a builder to construct your dream home, you need to provide a complete set of blueprints. To get a set of blueprints, you would have to spend a fair amount of time imagining the layouts, designs, and colors. You would engage a draftsman or architect to transform the image in your mind to the blueprints. How do you this? Mostly with your words.

Think about flower seed packets for a moment. A colorful picture of the flowers is usually featured front and center on the face of the packet—not the seeds. The sellers of the seeds are proactive and show you the possibilities of what can happen once you plant the seeds as recommended. You can take a similar approach when you visualize the possibilities of your dreams by drawing or printing a picture of your desires. If you visualize yourself being free of any debt, print a copy of your loan statements reflecting zero balances—and look at them often!

Before visualization, it is important to get very clear about what you want manifested or want to become. Nowadays, selfies are popular. When you visualize, be sure to include an image of yourself. To intensify the reality of your visualization experience, use all of your senses, including your feelings. This is similar to a driver setting out on a journey who gets the detailed address and description of the destination. After clarity on his destination, the driver determines the best ways to get there.

You can benefit from clearly visualizing your dreams and aspirational wonders. Before you get on the path to achieving your dreams, consider a few of the best ways to reach them. The meanings you convey with the words you speak should line up with the ways to achieve your dreams. Be sure to choose only words that cultivate and serve the best interests of your dreams. Speak these words aloud. Why aloud? When you speak aloud, you use more than one hundred laryngeal, orofacial, and respiratory muscles, seventy parts of your body, and sound waves that produce kinetic energy.

Energy promotes growth of whatever has been planted—good or bad. This is evident in seed growth since the seed produces after itself. For this reason, I have been advocating positive thoughts that give birth to positive dreams to grow within the "seed coat" of your heart. They photosynthesize from the energy of your spoken words. Your words have the ability to spur breakthrough growth from an internal image to reality.

Plan in Order to Do

Now that you have a clear picture and solid understanding of what you would like to achieve, the next step is to prudently plan the actions that line up with getting to the destination.

Proper planning provides direction and increases the possibility of assured achievement. It is absolutely worth the investment to sit down and complete your plan, which essentially is the foundation of your world-class desires.

As a part of completing your plan, ponder the execution of the activities. What is it going to take to be successful? What will you need to give? What will you need to give up? What words and meanings do you have to dig up? What foundational meanings for new words need to be laid? Consider your responses to the aforementioned questions carefully, thoughtfully, and deliberately. This assessment is an essential investment before you start taking steps toward your destinations.

This plan should be referred to frequently and should serve as a guiding star to your true north.

Strength by Action

By now, I hope you have decided to think in positive ways so you can interpret and attach meanings to words differently—and ultimately influence the actions you take. How do you keep this going and make a meaningful difference over time? After being willing to change, you accumulate strength by taking repeated actions over a period of time. Once you are on the move, it will be hard to stop you.

Behavioral scientist Dr. B. J. Fogg developed the Fogg Behavior Model to illustrate that when motivation, ability, and trigger components occur at the same time, the result is a behavior.[2] If one of the components is missing, a behavior will not occur. To illustrate this point, let me propose to pay you $50 million to fly from your continent to another continent once per week for the next month, using only your physical body. Even though the quantum of the payment might be highly motivational, given your lack of ability to fly, you will not be able to perform this action. Therefore, no behavior. If I made it easy for you by asking you to fly to the continents by jet (ability), paying (trigger) for your tickets, and making clear the itinerary, I am almost certain that you would readily get to the airport at the designated departure times and fly!

Because charity begins at home, I would encourage you to begin with the results of your self-reflection recommended in chapter 10 and determine the way you will change your self-talk to help you reach your dreams and goals in life. This could mean changing your self-talk to comprise of words with more positive meanings attached to them. Do this by, for example, repeating just one positive phrase daily. Identify an event that occurs in your daily life (for example, waking up in the morning, the sound of your alarm clock in the morning, or turning on the showerhead) and say the positive phrase after the event occurs. If you repeat this daily, you will gain momentum. These positive phrases are often called affirmations, from Latin *affirmare,* which means "to strengthen."

Performing this behavior daily for several days paves the way for this kind of self-talk to become a habit. When this one phrase becomes a habit, add another one. Continue this process to move forward along the pathway to your destinations. Consider the speed an airplane reaches just prior to takeoff or the growth in a plant or tree as it absorbs energy before producing fruits. Incremental increases strengthen motivation and build momentum for dynamic growth.

Author Gretchen Rubin seized the essence of habits when she said:

> Habits have a tremendous role to play in creating an atmosphere of growth, because they help us make consistent, reliable progress. ... Habit is notorious—and rightly so—for its ability to

direct our actions, even against our will; but by mindfully shaping our habits, we can harness the power of mindlessness as a sweeping force for serenity, energy, and growth.[3]

Wonder, Appreciation, and Reflection

Recap

With your words, you have a say in the pace and direction of the changes you desire. Visualization is a powerful ally on your journey, and it promotes alignment, unity, and action. Proper planning increases the likelihood of success.

Reflection

- You are constantly changing, and you can play a role in shaping this change. You can energize words to fulfill the images of your future.
- Start picturing your future with exhilaration. Bear in mind that, without a script, you will have nothing to produce.
- Based on all you have read and pondered in this book, reflect on your major insights so far regarding your wonderful, world-class future. With your words at center stage, step up and become the best writer, director, and producer of your life story.

Notes

_____

_____

_____

_____

_____

_____

_____

_____

_____

_____

_____

_____

_____

_____

_____

_____

_____

_____

_____

_____

_____

_____

_____

_____

_____

_____

_____

_____

_____

Chapter 14

Stay Put

To make real change, you have to be well anchored—not only in the belief that it can be done, but also in some pretty real ways about who you are and what you can do.

—Twyla Tharp

URING A TELEVISION PROGRAM BREAK, a teenager impatiently paced back and forth in the kitchen. The thirty-second countdown on the microwave seemed like an eternity. Many music videos from recent decades reflect a more frenetic pace, shifting from scene to scene every few seconds. These are mere glimpses of the pace of activities in today's world.

Patience Is a Virtue

While you are waiting for your dreams to manifest from the positive words you have created and planted in your heart, let the words remain firmly planted. The reasons manifestations of your words might take longer are varied and legitimate. In other words, not all results will happen overnight. Removing the seed from the ground means that it is extracted from life support and will quickly die. Removing well-anchored words will result in a similar course for your dreams. Do not give up before the seed germinates. No matter what your expectations, remember that growth is a process. When conditions are favorable, the seed will germinate.

You remove your positive words when you:

- Talk more about how bad things are and how bad they will get. For example, job security for you means having an ownership stake in your company, but if you keep saying how unfair the company is and that it will never give you an opportunity for a promotion, then your meaning does not stand a chance of surviving.
- Say or do things that contradict the intentions of your words. For example, financial freedom for you means freedom from debts, so maxing out your credit cards and seeking new ones are highly contradictory.
- Permit others to nullify the meanings you have attached to your words. For example, honesty for you signifies speaking the truth at all times, but this changes each time you give in to friends that say white lies and bending the truth are acceptable.

To have results, your seed must remain in the ground. Keep your positive and productive words firmly in your heart where favorable conditions will spur germination and the eventual manifestations of your heart's desires.

Turning Over and Nurturing for Best Results

When your seed stays put and receives sufficient nutrients under the right conditions, it will experience a burst of activity and put down roots to anchor itself. In chapter 11, I encouraged the use of a framework that involves focusing your thoughts in positive ways intently and at length. Turning over your thoughts nourishes your meaningful words and promotes the growth process, which results in stronger roots.

Mulling over or deeply reflecting on your words in positive ways is one of the most effective ways of creating staying power, growth, and momentum. The larger your words grow and the more momentum they have, the harder it will be to stop them. This is why, for example, landing large cargo jets normally requires much more force than small passenger planes to bring them to a stop.

Mulling over your thoughts and words in negative ways will deplete the energy and nourishment required to keep your words alive. Worrying is not the kind of deep reflection I am recommending.

If you nurture your thoughts and words, you will see your heart's desires manifesting like plants and trees visibly growing above the ground. In addition to caring for your thoughts and words, get into the habit of putting them to use. Consider the number of people who have studied foreign languages in high school but are unable to ask basic questions because of lack of use or practice over the subsequent years. Use them or lose them. Cherish and protect—rather than neglecting—the word treasures you build up.

Robert Green Ingersoll highlighted the importance of growth:

> The mind cannot be securely anchored. If we do not advance, we go backward. If we do not grow, we decay. If we do not develop, we shrink and shrivel.[1]

Wonder, Appreciation, and Reflection

Recap

The exercise of patience is required as you wait for your dreams to manifest from the positive words you have created and planted in your heart. When your positive words remain in your heart and are nourished, they will cause a burst of growth and strengthening of roots for a firm anchor. Ongoing deep, positive reflections on your words will lead to more staying power, growth, and momentum.

Reflection

- The power of persistence and staying put have paid dividends for many over the years. Accumulating funds in a savings account requires the discipline of leaving the initial amount deposited and building on that foundation.
- Keep positive words firmly rooted in your heart and remember that frequent withdrawals can slow growth of the account and deplete your success to date.
- With regard to your word treasure, reflect on the penny challenge: If you took a penny and doubled its value each day, how much money would you have at the end of ten days?

Day	Value
1	$0.01
2	$0.02
3	$0.04
4	$0.08
5	$0.16

6	$0.32
7	$0.64
8	$1.28
9	$2.56
10	$5.12

Notes

Chapter 15

Protect Your Legacy

Kind words are a creative force, a power that concurs in
the building up of all that is good, and energy that showers
blessings upon the world.

— Lawrence G. Lovasik

A S MENTIONED IN THE OPENING chapter of this book, the
town of Masada, where the oldest seed to germinate
was discovered, was identified by UNESCO as a World
Heritage Site. It is interesting to note that the clauses of the
UNESCO World Heritage mission statement address awareness,
protection, and preservation of such sites, given their natural
and cultural values.

Protecting Your Seed

I spent almost thirty years of my life in the banking industry.
In my early years in the profession, I frequently marveled at

the seemingly indestructible nature of vaults: steel-reinforced concrete, thick steel doors, complex locks, and antitheft devices. These secure spaces were designed to protect valuable contents.

I have posited throughout this book that your words are like seeds. Your words are precious, especially your productive words. Your words seed positive habits, which can become positive values that require protection and preservation. When you invest time and energy in developing a trove of valuable words, you need to protect them. Let us take a lesson from the Norway government's protection of samples of the world's seeds.

F. William Engdahl reported on January 28, 2016, in *Global Research* that the Bill and Melinda Gates Foundation had decided to invest $30 million in a seed bank in Svalbard, Norway.[1] Other sponsors included DuPont/Pioneer Hi-Bred, Syngenta Foundation, and the Rockefeller Foundation. The seed bank in Svalbard contains the largest diversity of crops in the world. According to the *Economist*, it "is a backup for the world's 1,750 seed banks, storehouses of agricultural biodiversity."[2] The seed bank opened in 2008 and was constructed inside a mountain protected by a vault with "dual blast-proof doors with motion sensors, two airlocks, and walls of steel-reinforced concrete one meter thick."

Safeguard valuable words and meanings you have created by ensuring that they are firmly rooted in your heart. In practical terms, this means really getting a profound understanding of these words and meanings. Go beyond understanding based on logic and reasoning. Remind yourself of their importance to you. Believe and experience them through clear visualization and your senses. Reinforce your deep understanding by decisively focusing your thoughts on these meanings. If you repeat this process regularly (as outlined in the previous chapter) so that it becomes habit, the meanings will be triggered routinely and effortlessly.

Dig In or Disperse

In checking the record books, wonders of the world lists, and World Heritage Site lists, I did not see a record for the magnificent man-made structure the people of Shinar envisioned. What happened? They were given instructions to separate, go in different directions, and establish flourishing communities. However, because of the benefits emanating from their common language and familiar surroundings, they dug in and did not let go. These nomads from the east, who were likely tired of pulling up tent stakes, had finally discovered their crown jewel and had no intentions of moving again. The very thing they refused to release did not give them the power, freedom, and fame they so badly desired. Instead, their language became diverse, and because of subsequent confusion, they were ultimately dispersed to scattered locations. Their dreams withered and their wonder of the world was left unfinished.

Unity is often touted as the binding ingredient for success, but this is not the only way to achieve success. Sadly, these visionary people's tenacious attachment to their unity ended up being a death grip on their dreams. This is an apt example of the difference between *willing* and *willful* that I shared in chapter 9; they took a willful position to their detriment.

Dispersion, on the other hand, sometimes conveys a sense of loss and weakness. For seeds, however, this is not the case. The dispersion of seeds ensures their continuity! The instruction to the people of Shinar was to be fruitful and fill the earth. Evidently these people self-reflected, but they did not seek trusted feedback, which would have revealed their blind spots (see chapter 10).

The plain of Shinar was fertile, but there was an apparent scarcity of stone, which why they decided to make bricks. Yes, sticking together could have lightened the load, but too much of a good thing can be harmful. When too many seeds are sown in one place, overcrowding results. This means that the plants would likely not grow well because too many of them are competing for the limited resources in the soil. Dispersion of the people of Shinar, with one language, would have ensured their fruitful continuity.

When you deliberately do not follow or accept your own success plan repeatedly, disunity and confusion uproot your valuable investments. Here are a few examples: purposely doing something else to avoid completing your plan because of deception and other "voices," self-sabotaging actions, and ignoring helpful advice from others. Sometimes your diversion from the plan might not be deliberate, but you have the choice to get back on track. *Stay the course!* The following fable illustrates the point. A hungry tiger was following the trail of a deer, but he detected the scent of a rabbit and shifted direction (after all, rabbits are tastier). He soon became distracted by a mouse, and his tiring detour ended with the mouse safely in a hole—out of the tiger's reach. The tiger finished his day tired, angry, and hungry!

Equally damaging to your success is when you allow selfish pride and ambition to dominate your thinking and actions; disarray eventually sets in and productivity wanes.

To multiply, the seed needs to grow sufficiently in order to produce fruit, which in turn protects its seeds and creates the possibility for this cycle of fruitfulness to repeat itself.

Persistently Protect Your Dreams

Frequently striving for clarity and checking your progress will enable you to be aware of any additional steps or changes needed to reach your goals. Make adjustments along the way. I was astonished to learn that when airplanes fly from point

A to point B, they go off course more than 90 percent of the time. Pilots remain routinely alert to determine their positions and persistently make adjustments until they reach their destinations.

You might not notice how certain thoughts and feelings sneak in and take residence in your mind. The quicker you respond to these uninvited party crashers, the better. Do you let these crashers get comfortable and eat and drink all of your food and beverages—or do you show them to the door?

A few years ago, a commercial bank offered to provide a loan to a client to purchase a large parcel of land. A sales agreement was signed, but the closing of the sale was disrupted when another person claimed that the property belonged to him. He claimed that he was "residing" on the land for years and was farming the land. How dare these other people try to "deprive him" of his source of income? The squatter did not have the title to the land or permission to use the land. Unfortunately, the rightful owner of the land was not really attentive to activities on the land, and the squatter started claiming to have rights! These rights are the legal allowances to use the property and could, over a prolonged period of time, be converted to title to the land.

Before trespassers cause you untold nightmares, quick and resolute action must be taken: kick out any parasites from your mind's land forthwith!

When a foreign substance gets into an oyster's shell, to protect itself, the oyster surrounds and traps it. It does not waste time with this irritant! This defensive action by the oyster is natural. Over time, the oyster keeps secreting this protective coating, and—eventually—a valuable pearl is formed. Imagine that a certain crab protects itself by entering the shell of the oyster and lives off the oyster's food! When allowed to get comfortable, the crab can cause permanent damage to the oyster's gill, which is used for gathering food and breathing. You know what happens when you cannot breathe or eat.

Protect yourselves against party-crashing thoughts and feelings—and do not let them get comfortable in your mind.

Stubbornly Persist

Stubbornness and hardheadedness are often associated with negative perceptions of being unreasonable. There are, however, times when stubbornness is absolutely necessary in order to succeed in many areas of your lives. Okay, a nicer way to say it is "persistence pays off." Both convey the sense of not yielding or giving up easily. No matter what disappointments, monkey wrenches, talking behind your back, or spokes being put in your wheels, do not quit.

As you pursue your dreams and desires with positive words and meanings, the world around you is constantly changing. Your reaction? Adapt and choose to respond in ways to thrive and overcome any obstacles. The Navy SEALS mantra says, "I accept the responsibility of my chosen profession ... I will never quit ... I persevere and thrive on adversity. If knocked down, I will get back up, every time."

Even if you slip and fall, get back up because the fall is temporary. Robert Brault captured this sentiment well when he said, "Stubbornly persist, and you will find that the limits of your stubbornness go well beyond the stubbornness of your limits."

Wonder, Appreciation, and Reflection

Recap

Your investment in accumulating productive words is worth your secure protection of them. Sharing these productive words and ways is great way to ensure fruitful continuity. Be persistent in your pursuit of success.

Reflection

- You are full of hidden treasures, including your meaningful words, which have incalculable intrinsic and extrinsic values. These treasures belong to you. Securely guard and protect them in your heart (your mind).
- As you start to experience the joy of having these treasures, reflect on some things you would like to create and preserve for others and future generations.
- How will your meaningful words be planted to multiply value for others?

Notes

_____

_____

_____

_____

_____

_____

_____

_____

_____

_____

_____

_____

_____

_____

_____

_____

_____

_____

_____

_____

_____

_____

_____

_____

_____

_____

_____

_____

_____

_____

Closing Words

One can choose to go back toward safety or forward toward growth. Growth must be chosen again and again; fear must be overcome again and again.

—Abraham Maslow

A s I LISTENED TO THE music on my iPod and pushed through exercises on the elliptical machine, I noticed a stepladder with a sticker with the word *danger*. A sign on the top said, "This is not a step." This piqued my curiosity, and I thought, *This must mean that every other rung below it is meant for you to step higher.* If you are not at *your* top, continue stepping up again and again.

Taking Action to Stay Above Ground

Positive action is required to break through your seed coats and climb to the top. Here are a few key ways to ensure that your climb is safe and fruitful:

- Choose the right ladder. It is pointless to use a stepladder to reach the top of a two-story house. To realize your dreams, it is important to choose the right ladder. Choose the best ways to achieve your dreams and desires. Is my action going to get me to my desired destination in a reasonable time? Deliberately pondering one positive thought every other day might be fine if you have hit your stride and have momentum that produces multiple successes daily. However, if your negative thoughts are taking over your life and destroying your fruitfulness, the frequency of one positive thought every other day would not likely be the right approach.

- Position the ladder at the proper angle. The position is important to prevent the feet of the ladder from slipping backward and the top of the ladder from sliding down. Before executing your various activities, it is worthwhile to properly position your feet (values, beliefs, attitudes, passion, and desires), reinforce this with your top (mind), and mind the slant of your thoughts and spoken words.

- Climb the ladder. Once you are in a position to move up—even though you might feel quite comfortable at ground level—you need to act. Once you know where you are going, you need to get going! Step on the first rung to make sure it will hold your weight—and then keep stepping up. Once you're in your car, drive. Once you're at work, work. In other words, do what's necessary to move forward and upward.

You can reach your full potential by frequently crossing your Ts as you move up in altitude with a positive attitude. Baseball Hall of Famer and World Series champion Wade Boggs expressed the power of this kind of attitude when he said, "A positive attitude causes a chain reaction of positive thoughts, events, and outcomes. It is a catalyst, and it sparks extraordinary results."

Preparing to Stretch

The *Oxford Dictionary* defines stretching as "Causing (someone) to make maximum use of their talents or abilities."[1]

When you do something often and consistently, habits form. The crux of the matter is that you make choices that fundamentally determine how your future will unfold. Stepping outside of your comfort zone, although difficult at times, can result in growth beyond your expectations. Sometimes you are motivated to step outside, but you quickly retreat when it becomes uncomfortable.

When the butterfly breaks out of the comfort of its cocoon, it does not try to get back in because of the discomfort of the external elements. Robin S. Sharma said, "I'd rather be willing to experiment with life and make a few mistakes than forego growth by refusing to step outside the confines of my comfort zone."[2] Within your comfort zones, you *rarely* reach your full potential and get a sense of meaningful fulfillment. In *How Successful People Think*, John Maxwell said, "When you find a place to *stretch* [emphasis added] your thoughts, you find that potential."[3]

As a teenager, I learned quickly the power of the rubber band, especially when it was properly connected as a part of a slingshot. I would firmly attach each end of the long, thick rubber band to the Y-shaped wire clothes hanger (the rubber band was threaded through a small piece of hard cardboard). As I reflect on the stretching power of the rubber band, I recall small stones being catapulted toward targets lined up on our vertical boundary wall. Stretching is not always bad. In fact, many of you are most effective when you are stretched.

Despite the awesome potential that can be achieved through being stretched, there is often a temptation to retreat or snap back to your comfort zone. In other words, there is a tendency to go back to old habits and business as usual. If you continue to hold on when being stretched, you will gradually grow like the rubber band and extend to a new size—a bigger person.

Commitment

A university student in his late teenage years was in search of employment. He was attracted to a job posting for a custodian. He figured that he could be a great caretaker. As he examined the job description, however, an unexpected picture emerged: cleaning bathrooms, sweeping, mopping, and waxing floors, and emptying and disposing of trash.

He got the position, showed up 100 percent every day on time, and carried out his responsibilities diligently. A short time later, an assistant manager position became available in the same building. Based on his work ethic, he was offered this higher-paying position and effectively had "custodial" responsibilities for the operations of that very building that he was instrumental in maintaining.

Consider a few suggestions that contributed to this student's successes and can help you as you push outside of your comfort zones.

- *Choose to act.* It is beneficial to get into the habit of doing necessary and sometimes difficult tasks right away. This means you take on the mind-set of resolving issues quickly and not waiting around for the magic to happen. Taking this key step and continuing could pave the way for many breakthroughs and opportunities. Nike promoted this impulsion to act and have a can-do attitude with its tagline "Just do it."

- *Do your very best where you are with what you have.* Perfect alignment of the stars is rare—so do your absolute best in your current circumstances. This approach and diligence will pay dividends over and over again. Adopting this approach on a consistent basis will contribute to your growth as a reliable custodian. Spencer West (a motivational speaker with the Free the Children Foundation) lost both legs from the pelvis at age five, yet he successfully climbed Mount Kilimanjaro (the highest mountain in Africa at 19,341 feet above sea level) on his hands and in his wheelchair in May 2012!

- *Be a fruitful custodian.* A biblical story was told about three guys who were given custody of three different amounts of money for a long time. Two of them were applauded for protecting the principal amount and wisely investing to generate double the original amounts in dividends/returns. Guess what? They were given more! The third guy—who had been entrusted with the least amount of money—complained that the boss (company) was hard and overly demanding. He was not about to take any chances. I suspect he griped throughout this time and later demonstrated to the boss that he kept the exact amount that was placed in his custody. Guess what? The money was taken away from him, and he was sent packing!

Promote rapid growth spurts of your dreams and desires by acting quickly with intention. Dare to step outside of your comfort zones. In your current circumstances, commit your energies and actions to results. Produce value appreciation in what you do and who you are—and then share and enjoy the fruits of your success!

Having a Say in Your Destiny

Seeds have growth power on the inside, and once the conditions are right, they grow and multiply. The fruits produced correlate invariably to the miniature plant on the inside of the seed. Your experiences in life correlate similarly to the words you speak to yourself and others. Your words literally have power when spoken (kinetic energy and mass in motion). They have the power to transport your thoughts, dreams, and desires from the hidden depths of your heart into the spotlight for your benefit and the benefit of others.

Use your word power wisely. Disperse them well. Engage your words as the chief carrier of beneficial meanings for you and others.

- Use your words to navigate your thoughts and seed productivity.
- Use your words to underwrite your dreams and protect yourself on the way to your destiny.
- Use your words to energize and transport you to your destiny—your wonder of the world.

Carpe Diem

Today I am calling on you to take action. Carpe literally means "to pluck," especially when picking fruit. *Pluck* suggests acting quickly to enjoy the fruits today since our time on earth is relatively short. There are some low-hanging fruits within your reach that you could pick without much effort—pluck them.

If you have diligently read up to this point, you have a lot of pluck! This means you have a strong will and desire to succeed. Carpe diem!

Notes

Chapter 1
Priceless

1. Kerry A. Dolan and Luisa Kroll, "Inside the 2015 Forbes 400: Facts and Figures About America's Wealthiest," *Forbes,* September 29, 2015, http://www.forbes.com/sites/luisakroll/2015/09/29/inside-the-2015-forbes-400-facts-and-figures-about-americas-wealthiest/#6aefc18928f8 (accessed July 21, 2016).

2. Rose Eveleth, "There are 37.2 Trillion Cells in Your Body: You know that your body is made of cells—But just how many? Turns out that question isn't all that easy to answer," *Smithsonian.com— Smart News,* October 24, 2013, http://www.smithsonianmag.com/smart-news/there-are-372-trillion-cells-in-your-body-4941473/ (accessed July 21, 2016).

3. "How Much Does Stem Cell Therapy Cost?" *Howmuchisit.org*, http://www.howmuchisit.org/stem-cell-therapy-cost/ (accessed July 21 2016).

4. Jay Hart, "Nadia Comăneci's Perfect 10 in Montreal," *Yahoo Sports*, June 28, 2012, https://ca.sports.yahoo.com/news/olympics-olympics-montreal-nadias-perfect-10.html (accessed July 21, 2016).

5. Simon Burnton, "50 Stunning Olympic Moments No. 5: Nadia Comaneci Scores a Perfect 10," *The Guardian*, December 14, 2011, https://www.theguardian.com/sport/london-2012-olympics-blog/2011/dec/14/50-olympic-moments-nadia-comaneci (accessed July 21, 2016).

6. Werner Gitt, "Information: The Third Fundamental Quantity," *Siemens Review* (November/December 1989): 56:2–7.

7. Giorgio Vasari, *Lives of the Most Eminent Painters, Sculptors and Architects* (London: Philip Lee Warner, 1912–15), 14.

Chapter 2
World-Class Potential

1. "The Seven Wonders of the Ancient World," *Seven-wonders-world. com*, http://www.seven-wonders-world.com/ (accessed July 22, 2016).

2. "World Heritage List: Masada," *UNESCO.org*, http://whc.unesco.org/en/list/1040/ (accessed July 22, 2016).

3. Steven Erlanger, "After 2,000 Years, a Seed From Ancient Judea Sprouts," *The New York Times*, June 12, 2005, http://www.nytimes.com/2005/06/12/world/middleeast/after-2000-years-a-seed-from-ancient-judea-sprouts.html?_r=0 (accessed July 22, 2016).

4. "Oldest Seed Germinated," *Guinness World Records*, http://www.guinnessworldrecords.com/world-records/oldest-seed-germinated/ (accessed July 22, 2016).

5. "Internet Usage Statistics: The Internet Big Picture," *Internet World Stats*, http://www.internetworldstats.com/stats.htm (accessed July 25, 2016).

6. Gary Keller and Jay Papasan, *The One Thing: The Surprisingly Simple Truth Behind Extraordinary Results* (London: Hodder and Stoughton, 2013), 11.

Chapter 3
New Beginnings

1. Julie Huynh, "Study Finds No Difference in the Amount Men and Women Talk," *Gazette*, University of Arizona, June 19, 2014, https://ubrp.arizona.edu/study-finds-no-difference-in-the-amount-men-and-women-talk/ (accessed July 23, 2016).
2. Oxford Dictionaries, s.vv. "the fruits or the fruit," http://www.oxforddictionaries.com/definition/english/fruit (accessed July 23, 2016).
3. "Linguistics may be clue to emotions, according to Penn State research," *PennState/News*, January 20, 2005, http://news.psu.edu/story/212528/2005/01/20/linguistics-may-be-clue-emotions-according-penn-state-research (accessed July 23, 2016).

Chapter 4
Choices and Spin-Off Benefits

1. Betty Hart and Todd R. Risley, "The Early Catastrophe: The 30 Million Word Gap by Age 3," *American Educator* (Spring 2003), 4–9.

Chapter 5
Three Sides to Every Story

1. C. K. Ogden and I. A. Richards, *The Meaning of Meaning* (Orlando: Harcourt Brace Jovanovich, Inc. 1989), 10–12.
2. "Highest Insurance Value for a Painting," *Guinness World Records*, December 14, 1962, http://www.guinnessworldrecords.com/world-records/highest-insurance-valuation-for-a-painting (accessed July 23, 2016).

3. Bruce Davis, "There Are 50,000 Thoughts Standing Between You and Your Partner Every Day!" *The Huffington Post: The Blog*, May 23, 2013 (updated July 23, 2013), http://www.huffingtonpost.com/bruce-davis-phd/healthy-relationships_b _3307916.html (accessed July 23, 2016).

Chapter 7
Harness Your Power

1. Patrick Kevin Day, "Nik Wallenda's high-wire walk, Jesus talk revs up Twitter." *Los Angeles Times*, June 24, 2013, http://www.latimes.com/entertainment/tv/showtracker/la-et-st-nik-wallenda-high-wire-jesus-twitter-20130624-story.html (accessed July 23, 2016).
2. "Grand Canyon Crossed by Tightrope Walker," *Sky News*, September 19, 2013, http://news.sky.com/story/grand-canyon-crossed-by-tightrope-walker-10442141 (accessed July 23, 2016).
3. Collins English Dictionary, s.v. "harness," http://www.collinsdictionary.com/dictionary/english/harness (accessed July 23, 2016).

Chapter 8
Choose to Be a Friend of Your Destiny

1. Proverbs 27:17 (New Living Translation).
2. "MLK Quote of the Week: Faith is taking the First Step …," *The King Center*, http://www.thekingcenter.org/blog/mlk-quote-week-faith-taking-first-step (accessed July 23, 2016).
3. Numbers 13, 14 (New American Standard Bible).

Chapter 9
Infuse Power in Your Words

1. "Personal Triumph of Team USA Goalkeeper Tim Howard," *ABC News: World News with David Muir* (aired June 22, 2014).
2. Ed Payne and Steve Almasy, "10 Surprising Facts about America's New Soccer Hero, Tim Howard," *CNN*, July 2, 2014, http://edition.

cnn.com/2014/07/01/sport/football/tim-howard-spotlight/index.html (accessed July 24, 2016).

3. William Grimes, "Amos Ferguson, 89, Bahamian Artist, Is Dead," *The New York Times*, October 29, 2009, http://www.nytimes.com/2009/10/30/arts/design/30ferguson.html?_r=0 (accessed July 24, 2016).

4. "Artist Biography: Amos Ferguson," *The National Art Gallery of The Bahamas (NAGB)*, September 20, 2012, http://nagb.org.bs/mixedmediablog/2012/09/artist-biography-amos-ferguson.html?rq=amos%20ferguson (accessed July 24, 2016).

5. "Most dominoes toppled by an individual," *Guinness World Records*, December 31, 2011, http://www.guinnessworldrecords.com/world-records/most-dominoes-toppled-by-an-individual (accessed July 26, 2016).

Chapter 10
Treat Yourself to a Makeover

1. Tiffany A. Ito, Jeff T. Larsen, N. Kyle Smith, and John T. Cacioppo, "Negative Information Weighs More Heavily on the Brain: The Negativity Bias in Evaluative Categorizations," *Journal of Personality and Social Psychology* 75, no. 4 (1998): 887–900.

2. John T. Cacioppo, Tanya L. Chartrand, Heather A. Katafiasz, Jeff T. Larsen, Kathleen E. Moran, and N. Kyle Smith, "Being Bad Isn't Always Good: Affective Context Moderates the Attention Bias Toward Negative Information," *Journal of Personality and Social Psychology* 90, no. 2 (2006): 210–220.

Chapter 11
Discover Your Think Tank

1. Thomas More, *Four Last Things: The Supplication of Souls. A Dialogue on Conscience* (New York: Scepter Publishers, 2002), 21.

2. Philippians 4: 8 (New Living Translation).

3. Jennifer Warner, "Words Really Do Hurt: Study Shows Words Alone May Activate Pain Response in the Brain," *WebMD Health*

News, April 2, 2010, http://www.webmd.com/pain-management/news/20100402/words-really-do-hurt (accessed July 24, 2016).

4. Barbara L. Fredrickson, *Positivity: Top-Notch Research Reveals the 3 to 1 Ratio That Will Change Your Life* (New York: Three Rivers Press, 2009), 10–11.

Chapter 12
Design and Build Your World

1. *Encyclopedia.com: Encyclopedia of World Biography*, s.v. "Christiansen, Ole Kirk," http://www.encyclopedia.com/doc/1G2-2506300044.html (accessed July 24, 2016).

2. "The Lego Group," *Lego.com*, http://www.lego.com/en-us/aboutus/lego-group (accessed July 24, 2016).

3. "Tallest structure built with Lego®," *Guinness World Records*, June 21, 2015, http://www.guinnessworldrecords.com/world-records/tallest-structure-built-with-interlocking-plastic-bricks (accessed July 24, 2016).

4. "Largest caravan built with interlocking plastic bricks," *Guinness World Records*, October 8, 2015, http://www.guinnessworldrecords.com/world-records/379659-largest-caravan%c2%a0built-with-interlocking-plastic-bricks (accessed July 24, 2016).

5. "Largest Great Ball Contraption," *Guinness World Records*, June 27, 2015, http://www.guinnessworldrecords.com/world-records/381549-largest-great-ball-contraption (accessed July 24, 2016).

6. "Thoughts That Win," *Association for Psychological Science*, May 25, 2011, http://www.psychologicalscience.org/index.php/news/releases/thoughts-that-win.html (accessed July 24, 2016).

Chapter 13
Change for Better

1. Genesis 11:1–9 (New International Version).
2. B. J. Fogg, "What Causes Behavior Change," *behaviormodel.org*, http://www.behaviormodel.org/ (accessed July 24, 2016).
3. Gretchen Rubin, *Better Than Before: Mastering the Habits of Our Everyday Lives* (Canada: Anchor Canada, 2015), 12.

Chapter 14
Stay Put

1. Robert G. Ingersoll, *The Works of Robert G. Ingersoll, Vol. 4 (of 12),* (New York: the Dresden Publishing Co., 1902), 7.

Chapter 15
Protect Your Legacy

1. F. William Engdahl, "'Doomsday Seed Vault' in the Arctic," *Global Research*, January 28, 2016, http://www.globalresearch.ca/doomsday-seed-vault-in-the-arctic-2/23503 (accessed July 24, 2016).
2. "Banking against Doomsday," *Economist*, May 10, 2012, http://www.economist.com/node/21549931 (accessed July 24, 2016).

Closing Words

1. Oxford Dictionaries, s.v. "stretch," http://www.oxforddictionaries.com/definition/english/fruit (accessed July 24, 2016).
2. Robin Sharma, *Discover Your Destiny: Big Ideas to Live Your Best Life* (New York: HarperCollins, 2006), 42.
3. John C. Maxwell, *How Successful People Think: Change Your Thinking, Change Your Life* (New York: Center Street, 2009), xvii.

Printed in the United States
By Bookmasters